The Art of The Builder

Elevating Construction Senior Superintendents
- Book 1 -
The Leader and the Team

A Principle Based Leadership Guide for Project, Senior, and General Superintendents in Construction using the Integrated Production Control System

Copyright © 2022 Jason Schroeder
All rights reserved
ISBN: 9798841694984
Imprint: Independently published

Elevating Construction Senior Superintendents

Written by Jason Schroeder

Edited by Joan Willden

Acknowledgements

We had quite a team reviewing this work before it was published. It was so well reviewed I was shocked at the standard the reviewers were setting. I remember telling my wife, Kate, "I don't know if I can do this. I'm not a good enough writer." Obviously, she told me to "cowboy up," and the reviewers and editors helped me along. So I want to give a few shout-outs as we begin.

I want to shout-out Hensel Phelps for training me to be a builder, DPR Construction for giving me the time and the opportunity to learn and implement lean techniques on projects, and Okland Construction for trusting me to implement these across dozens of projects with them. I would not be here today without working with such dynamic companies.

Joel Hamilton

So, my first thanks goes to a proud, Albertan rodbuster and ironworker with vast construction experience. Joel has been a part of projects that have ranged from heavy industrial in Alberta's oil fields to ornamental fences and handrails in Canada's North West Territories and deep metro stations and tunnels in Montreal, Quebec. Joel has also overseen large-scale, stair and rail packages in Metropolitan, New York to mall and greenhouse renovations in Edmonton, Alberta. Joel brings hands-on, boots-on-the-ground field experience and practical education (BBA, NCSO) to his current role as a Senior Project Manager for EZ Steel and as a member of the Camnor Group (a group of steel companies located in Alberta and Quebec, Canada). When Joel isn't managing steel construction, he and his wife, Sarah, are building the Hamilton Homestead surrounded by their four kids and their gaggle of animals on the outskirts of Leduc, AB. He enjoys volunteering within their community and church as well. An avid audiobook 'reader', daily podcast listener and content-consumer of my content from the early days of the Elevate Podcast, Joel is deeply honored to have the opportunity to join the Elevate Team in the creation of Art of The Builder: Elevating Construction Senior Superintendents - Book 1 - The Team and the Leader.

Here is a quote directly from Joel: "When you meditate and apply the principles that Jason lays out in the forthcoming pages, you will elevate your abilities and leadership from building projects to building builders. Thank you for coming on this journey of self and Jobsite improvement with us. I know what lies ahead will grow you and impact your career in ways few books have done before. On we go." - Joel Hamilton

Boone White

Boone was raised on a farm in rural Mississippi. He graduated from the University of Southern Mississippi in 2008 and went on to work for Hoar Construction, LLC as an assistant superintendent where he had the opportunity to work on several different types and sizes of projects all over the country and gained a well-rounded knowledge base of building. Boone's career was forever changed in 2015 when he was introduced to Lean after reading The Goal and 2 Second Lean. Shortly after that, he learned The Last Planner System and helped implement it on several projects. From that, Boone's heart was changed in a way that drives him to find better ways to build projects with respect for people. In 2019, Boone and his family decided to move back to his hometown of Oxford, MS and join ICM Construction. Boone has been charged with implementing Lean concepts and practices throughout the company, but his goal is to eventually impact and improve the construction industry in Mississippi and the surrounding states.

Dan Fauchier

Dan Fauchier, CMF is a Certified Master Facilitator for Lean Development, Design and Construction, with 42 year's experience. He is co-author of a recent book with David Umstot, Lean Project Delivery: Building Championship Project Teams, available on Amazon.com. With Thais Alves, PhD, SDSU, Dan co-authored peer-reviewed IGLC academic papers "Last Planner® System: Gateway to Lean Behaviors" and with Alves and David Umstot, "Metrics of Public Owner Success in Lean Design, Construction, and Facilities Operations and Maintenance". For Construction Accelerator® (www.tryCAnow.com) Dan produces, co-writes and co-presents 3-9 minute lean training videos.

I want to say, "Thank you," to these wonderful men who reviewed this book and helped me get it out to our beloved industry. - Jason

Dedication

This book is dedicated to the development of people. To quote a saying I really like, "Until we get that it is about people, we don't get it." It really is all about people—which is why I think it's very appropriate that the first book for general, senior, and project superintendents begins with team balance and health. It's about the people on the team. The first part of the next book for senior superintendents will be about how a good team of people can treat the other people on the project and operate project systems together.

Let me tell you a story to illustrate why book 1 needed to be people and team focused. I was once courted by a company to help improve field operations and lead efforts to improve all field positions. After a remarkable series of meetings, I thought I was in complete alignment with the vision and core values of this company. I hired on and helped them train their builders, set up development programs, and structure their departments. It went very well until there was an ever-so-slight shift in priority. As soon as the company leaders began seeing the results, they turned their attention to more sales, improved technology, and more processes and procedures. Additionally, they put a stop to a number of training programs that offered personal and professional development for their employees because they felt they had gone far enough. It didn't take long before I noticed this drift and made it clear that I would no longer work with them. When we parted ways, I remember feeling they cared only about the company, money, and their clients, and that people came second. So I fired them.

After my departure, I spoke with an old friend and mentor who summed up the situation nicely. He said, "Jason, they lured you in with a promise to bless people and later focused only on the process without the promise made to the people." It hit me. To them, people were tools, numbers, and things that were expendable. People were not first to them; the job, customer, and business was first. Interestingly, once they took this turn their processes and results began to suffer.

People come first. People run your business. People continuously improve your business. And, oh yeah, people are the only things we can take with us in this life and the next. I want you to know I will never again make the mistake of working with an organization or team that only wants process without the promise of people. My dedication is to everyone in our wonderful industry who works to support their own family, who knows employees and people come before clients and profits, and who knows remarkable projects are run by remarkable people and teams. To you I say, "Thank you," and "I love you." You make our industry fun, exciting, and wonderful. It is also wonderful to report that I get to work continuously with a number of people and companies like this. Their teams are happy, and their companies are thriving. Remember, until we get that it is about people, we don't get it.

Table of Contents

Acknowledgements i
Dedication v
Preface by Jason Schroeder 9

Introduction 13
  Giving 13
  Desire 15
  Morality and Ethics 18
  Leading vs. Doing...19
  Book Outline...21

The Captain..25
Key 1 - Teams are Working - (Build the Team) 26
Key 2 - People are Trained -
(Create Capability and Capacity) 27
Key 3 - Keep the Ship Properly Stocked - (Logistics) 28
Key 4 - Maintain the Ship's Systems - (Operations) 30
Key 5 - You Know Where You Are Going -
(Strategic Planning) 31
Key 6 - Everyone Knows How to Get There -
(Short-Interval Planning) 33
Key 7 - Keep the Ship Afloat (Project Controls) 34

Part 1 - Team Balance and Health............................37
  Your Motive 38
  The Five Behaviors 42

The Big Three - Team Development 60
The Phases of Team Development 65
Building Team Capacity 68
Remarkable Communication 90
Rules of Thumb When Building a Team: 99
Jobsite Support Ideas 101
An Interview with Ricky Davenport 103

Part 2 - The Leader 119

Success Habits -
(Developing The Leaders of This Journey) 121

The Success Formula -
(Doing The Right Things at The Right Time) 132

The Characteristics of Generals -
(Doing Things The Right Way) 151

The Blocks to Leadership - (Don't Be Held Back) 177

The 7 Deadly Sins -
(Don't Let Unlearned Skills Slow You Down) 184

Field Position Levels 195

General Superintendent Commandments 207

**General Superintendent Daily,
Weekly, and Monthly Tasks** 209

Project Audit 213
The Measurement of a Great Project 215

The Books 221

Conclusion 229

Preface by Jason Schroeder

My book, *Elevating Construction Superintendents*, lists tried and true, uncontroversial principles and steps any superintendent can follow to become more effective in their position. In a sense, it was an easy home run for me and for Elevate Construction. Accepting the concepts in that book is not difficult because people in the position of assistant superintendent and superintendent are still molding their style. This book is much more difficult because it describes advanced principles and steps that are shaped by style and form as well as experience. This book targets project, senior, and general superintendents. Most of the people reading this have already formed their habits and styles. This is a good thing, and it is to be expected. Consequently, we must approach this book differently.

I patterned this book after what was successful for me as I studied some of the best builders in my circles. You likely have your own systems, steps, and you certainly have your own style but you can absolutely adapt the principles in this book to fit your style. My greatest desire is that anyone in construction, whether college educated or not, whether English is their first language or not, and whether they have had the same opportunities or not, can succeed and go as far as they want. My second desire would be that the position of superintendent becomes elevated and universally equal with project management positions. I want supers on leadership teams, represented at all company levels, and showing up in all phases of construction. This is one of the ways to reverse our industry's productivity decline. To do that we need a new paradigm though.

The old way of finishing projects on time, by crash landing and burning people out does not help our industry or build people and families. And successful supers do not hurt people. Period. If we are ignorant of the consequences of, "just bringing it in on time," then we are doomed to a continual decline in our success and productivity as an industry. But if we double, triple, and quadruple our training and learning in construction and set ourselves on a path of continual progress, we will increase our ability to improve the lives of others. I can't think of another platform or venue more suited to bless more lives. Not in our churches, non-profits, associations, or social groups will we find more people ready to be served and blessed than in construction. In our spheres of personal influence construction is our mission, our service, and our ministry. Let's make the most of it.

The new way is to expect more and truly elevate ourselves and our industry. To do this we need to first build a foundation. We call this foundation: lean construction.

Below are the key concepts of lean construction.

Respect for People and Resources

A crucial concept from Paul Akers and the lean community, originating in Japanese culture, is the concept of respect for people and resources. In Japanese culture, they hold a great respect for people-even to the point of providing constant and life-long training and support at levels we would not even consider or believe in the United States. The Japanese consider the years between primary schooling and mid-life the golden years of a person's productivity. Many companies in Japan respect, appreciate, and acknowledge their employees and consider it a gift when employees work with their company during the "productive years."

Additionally, Japan is an island of limited resources whose inhabitants are constrained by a rice culture which relies on family and tradition. (Read Paul Akers' *Banish Sloppiness* to learn more.) In the United States, we hold a perception of unlimited resources and we don't show the same respect towards people. Don't believe me? I can prove it with one word. Bathrooms! In our industry, we disrespect countless workers day in and day out by providing unclean, unstocked, and insufficient bathrooms. This kind of disrespect permeates all other aspects of a construction project. So, if we want to get better, we will respect the resources we have and the people who use them. It is the only foundation upon which to build a Lean culture. The second concept is...

Creating Stable Environments with Flow that Bring Problems to the Surface

Nothing, and I do mean nothing, can ever be improved without stability. Yes, stability can begin once we are motivated by respect, but we will never progress unless we can stabilize our projects. That means cleanliness, organization, safety, operational excellence, and most importantly flow. Most of the construction industry does not flow and CPM scheduling is one of the biggest culprits. Ignorance is the other. Every part of our projects should flow, and the trades should flow nicely from area to area. When we flow as a stable project, worker counts, material inventory, and costs all reduce, and profits increase. Additionally, and most importantly, problems rise to the surface so they can be removed to make work ready. You will never improve anything without flow. You will never flow without stability. Once you have stability you can gain...

Total Participation with Visual Systems

The industry largely ignores the workers on construction projects by failing to provide training and orientation and then dispatching them into new and sometimes dangerous situations without explaining expectations or providing needed support systems. How much better would projects be if everyone received intense training, a detailed and effective orientation, and were a part of the planning of the work in a visual way? On our projects there may only be one to twelve leaders. Why not make that thirty or one hundred or three hundred by connecting, leveraging, and listening to everyone and rallying them to our cause? What if everyone was headed in the same direction? What if everyone knew how to behave safely within our project culture? What if everyone knew how to care for the owner? What if we all participated together? The answer is that things would be remarkable if that happened. It must be done. What you are looking for is an environment where everyone sees as a group, knows as a group, and acts like a group. Without that, we make no progress. The last concept is...

Quality Work and Continuous Improvement that Meets a Customer Need

With respect, stability, and total participation we can improve work and accomplish our mission of building people and families. Without them, we are spinning our wheels. Once everyone is brought into a stable and respectful system and we have total participation, we can improve, achieve our production targets, and increase the productivity and efficiency of construction as a whole to produce what customers order—an end product with good service.

These four concepts are the basis of lean construction. They will provide a footing upon which to build remarkable projects. If we build our projects with these four concepts, and in the order prescribed, we will move from the old way of just finishing on time to finishing with quality, safety, cost, a happy team, a raving fan owner, and people who are learning and progressing along the way.

Introduction

I want to personally welcome you to the book *Elevating Construction Senior Superintendents!* We are about to take an amazing, albeit difficult journey together where we discover the best way to control our environments through remarkable cultures and phenomenal systems. We are about to become the Navy Seals of construction. We are going to be the best in the business. The role of a superintendent isn't easy, but expanding your education will gain you the skill and expertise to run and replicate success on every project you lead. We will begin with a few principles that govern the rest of the book like general notes or specifications precede and govern all other plan views and details in a set of plans. Everything we discuss in this book should be implemented with these in mind.

Giving

Giving is the core of happiness and fulfillment in life. As humans we tend to take rather than give. Retraining ourselves to be givers is not an easy task. For example, there is a training simulation we use in Lean circles called *Silent Squares*. I won't give away the simulation in its entirety in case you get the chance to be a part of it, but I can tell you a few things. First, a team of five is given five envelopes. In these envelopes, geometrically shaped pieces of cardstock are included. The teams are given the following rules:

1. No talking.
2. Each person's goal is to make a 6"x6" square with the shapes.

3. You cannot ask for a piece. The only way a person may pass a piece is to give it. There is no asking, pointing, grunting, hinting, or requesting of any kind. (I always add there is no telepathic communication or praying, to be funny.) The point is people cannot "take" a piece. it can only be given.
4. Begin.

The reflection that occurs when the game is over can be life-changing. At least it was for me. In every simulation I have been a part of, the participants are able to stay quiet throughout even amid the laughing and giggling, but every person inevitably puts their own interests ahead of their team's needs. Most participants grab a piece, point for a piece, or just take over the entire table of pieces. By my observation, the natural tendency is for humans to take when it would be much more beneficial to adjust our behaviors to do more giving, serving, and loving. To be a great leader, you must be a great giver. Some have said to me that these concepts sound silly and touchy-feely, but you will never be truly successful until you learn to be a giver and until your motive is service.

Heaven favors those who bless others, and takers always end up disappointed. As author Robert Kiyosaki said in his book, *Uncommon Advantage*, "The best business leaders establish themselves by giving and trust." The systems in this book will only work if you can focus on giving. For more information on this principle, I recommend the books, *The Go-Giver: A Little Story About a Powerful Business Idea* by Bob Burg and John David Mann or *The Leader Who Had No Title* by Robin Sharma. In order to focus on these concepts daily and rewire our brains, I strongly encourage a morning routine that centers on gratitude and giving. Without this, there is no daily reinforcement of the behaviors and beliefs.

Desire

Your life's direction is determined less by circumstance and more by your desires and the resulting actions. It is the guiding force for your life. Too many leaders in construction feel like they are victims of circumstance. They are not! They are victims of their desires. They are victims of their mental set points. They will get what they want at home and on the project. Why do projects fail? Is it because of circumstances? No! It is because desires are not aligned with success.

Whoever you are is what your project will be. If you are messy in your habits and beliefs, your project will be messy. If you are unsafe in your habits and beliefs, your project will be unsafe and so will everyone on your project. If you are late in your habits and beliefs, your project will be late. Your desires and mental set point will drive everything you do at work. Please stop for a moment and really take this in. I imagine many of you do not believe what I have just said, but I assure you it's true. The condition of your project is an exact replica of who you are because you are responsible! If you want to change it you can. However, it's possible you don't want to change it badly enough yet because you have not yet found your "why." Just as a thermostat will adjust the highs and lows of a room's temperature, your mental setpoint—what you have come to expect and want—will keep the project in balance and on target according to your mindset.

What can we do? You have to change your mindset! You have to change your desires! You have to raise your setpoint! I was on a project once where Joe, the plumbing foreman, came to me and said, "Jason, I finally understand you. You just want us to see things like you see them. You want us to rise to the level of your expectations." I cannot thank Joe enough for articulating this to me, because it is the secret to success. I cannot easily explain how you improve your setpoint, your desires, and your expectations other than to tell you how I have done it.

Here are some things I do:
1. I attend leadership conferences and experiences every year. I need the energy boost, and motivation from events like leadership breakthrough sessions, Tony Robbins events, or certification training. I would highly recommend this habit to you as well. Everyone needs a boost to increase their performance.
2. I read a book a week. Reading books constantly has been the single biggest value-add habit for me in my life because it educates me, expands my influence, and drives me to want more. If you learn nothing else from this book than to read other books, it will be well worth the money.
3. I learn about leaders, role models, and mentors. I remember back to the time when I first watched the movie, Patton. It was so good I also read a biography and did research to learn more. George S. Patton was a flawed character but arguably one of the most successful American military generals in history. I have patterned myself after his leadership with organization, cleanliness, and safety. I have similar thoughts about training, and my expectations are very high, as his were. We must have examples, mentors, and role-models that challenge us to do better and want more.
4. I have only been on successful projects. When I say that I have been accidentally successful I mean it. I have never been on a failed or struggling project, and I never mean to. Sure, I have recovered dozens and assisted others, but I have never been an integral team member on a bad project, and I do not

recommend you be either. If you get positioned on one in your early years, I would ask to be transferred immediately before you get used to it. If you have to help with one, let it end there. If you have to be a part of two, never let it become three. People on bad projects fall into a learned hopelessness and lower their mental setpoints. Everyone needs to work on multiple successful projects to elevate their expectations and desires.

Ultimately it is all about wanting more and expecting more. I run clean projects because I have trained myself to be a clean person. I desire transparent job sites because I have learned to be a transparent person. Things exist on our projects that we allow to exist. Your job reflects what you tolerate. If there is a lack of safety on the job, you expressly said it was okay. If there is a mess on-site, you authorized it. If the project is late, you said it was acceptable. Why do I say this? Because you are the god of this world. (I hope I didn't offend my religious friends with that. I spelled it with a lower-case "g" on purpose. I mean you are the earthly "god" of your world.) Everything is under the control of the general contractor, superintendent, and project manager teams. If you are not happy with your circumstances of performance, change your desires. I love this quote from the Scriptures: "To him it is given according to his desires, whether he desireth good or evil, life or death, joy or remorse of conscience." I would translate that to construction by saying, "To him it is given according to his desires, whether he desireth success or failure, winning, or losing, fulfillment or disappointment and anguish." And so it is with us. We get what we want and what we tolerate. It mostly comes down to our desires.

Morality and Ethics

While it may be hard for some to define morality and ethics and the subsequent standard, it should be a real consideration in all you do. An immoral leader will hurt more people than they help. An unethical leader will damage more than they build. I have learned over the years that procedures like morning worker huddles, team meetings, accountability, zero tolerance, and accountability systems only work if the leader cares about people and is moral and ethical. Basically, a virtuous system or tool does not work in the hands of an immoral and unethical leader.

A quick definition of morality:

From *The History of the World* by Will and Ariel Durrant, "Morality refers to the set of standards that enable people to live cooperatively in groups. It's what societies determine to be "right" and "acceptable." Sometimes, acting in a moral manner means individuals must sacrifice their own short-term interests to benefit society."

A quick definition of ethics:

Moral principles that govern a person's behavior or the conduct of an activity.

A moral and ethical leader will understand what is right and wrong and behave according to that understanding.

I once heard of a discussion with an on-site superintendent who told the team he once intentionally walked through a trade contractor's fresh concrete to prove a point. He was angry about a mess they had not cleaned up so he decided to "motivate" the crew by walking through their concrete placement. As he told this story, he was proud of his object lesson. Five attempts were made to try and explain to him why his action was disrespectful; he persisted in the belief that what he'd done was "right" because it was effective. After all, he got the crew to clean up their area and he also got their attention. Now obviously this superintendent's actions were rude, disrespectful, and totally unacceptable. He had no sense of right or wrong in his react ion. No system, process, method, or approach can elevate an unethical and immoral leader. Morals and ethics must be at the base of every system we will discuss in this book.

Leading vs. Doing

Leading as opposed to doing can be difficult to maneuver. As a supervisor, your primary role is to lead. Stop shoveling, sweeping, and performing basic work. Your job is to move head-first into the harder, more complex, and more difficult leadership tasks by executing the following five keys:

1. You build the team by caring for and respecting individuals.
2. You have difficult conversations.
3. You manage, coach, and mentor direct reports.
4. You ensure the team is holding effective and remarkable meetings.
5. You scale clarity and communication effectively.

That sounds easy right? Let's look at that list again! No, I mean really look at it. Here they are again. Great leaders do the following five things:

1. They build the team by caring and respecting individuals.
2. They have difficult conversations.
3. They manage, coach, and mentor direct reports.
4. They ensure the team is holding effective and remarkable meetings.
5. They scale clarity and communication effectively.

Those five things are gut-wrenchingly hard! In fact, most

leaders do not want to do them, and will abdicate their responsibility to avoid them. Building teams and dealing with people issues is complex, frustrating, and difficult. Having hard conversations, calling someone out, discussing an upsetting topic with the owner or tackling a touchy subject frightens even the most seasoned construction supervisor. Managing and coaching an employee seems possible until you have to tell them to be more punctual to meetings, improve their hygiene, or step up their performance. And holding an effective meeting on your project and effectively scaling clarity and communication is no easy task.

As a leader you get to do those difficult things, and you no longer do the easy things. If you are reading this book for your position, your easy days are over. Paperwork, quality checks, layout, using the total station, directing traffic in the field, and spending most of your time with the foremen are no longer your primary role. As a leader you get to go tackle all the problems no one else wants to tackle, and.... stay with me, this is the best part... every problem no one else *can* tackle. You get to do what no one else can or wants to do. You get to do the hard things. Working hard and being busy is what got you your leadership position. Now you must stop thinking your role is to work hard and stay busy. You must lead well and pause. You have to watch, observe, direct, communicate, organize, and spend enough time with each individual on your team to be effective. The people and teams you effectively lead with the five keys will accomplish the tasks you no longer do.

For more information on this, read *The Motive* by Patrick Lencioni. The question you have to answer when reading is, "Am I willing to do the things leaders do?" and "What is my motive for being a leader?" If you can answer those questions sincerely, you are ready to implement as a senior leader on your project.

I hope those four topics were personally helpful to you. I do want to say again that they are crucial to your success in your role. You will achieve very little without those as a foundation. What would you add to that list?

As you think about that, let me explain the...

Book Outline

This work will be separated into at least two books:

Book 1 - Elevating Construction Senior Superintendents - The Team and The Leader
Book 2 - Elevating Construction Senior Superintendents - The System

There is too much information to include in just one book. In this first book we will focus on the leader and the team.

Below is a preview of the entire system as it is separated into these two books:

The Integrated Production Control System:

Book 1:

Lean Principle: Respect for People & Resources

The Team

- Building High Performance Project Teams
- The Senior Superintendent Leader

Book 2 and beyond:

Lean Principle: Respect for People & Resources

The Team

- Winning Over and Respecting the Workforce
- Onboarding and Orientation

Lean Principle: Stability, Capability, Capacity, & Flow

Project Development
- Intentional Design and Preconstruction
- Takt Planning
- Setup Lean in Contracts
- Prefabrication

Lean Principle: Total Participation with Visual Systems

The Environment
- Remarkable Interaction Systems
- Logistics Systems
- The Meeting System
- Procurement and Deliveries

Lean Principle: Quality & Continuous Improvement that Meets a Customer Need

Accountability
- Quality Program
- Daily Correction
- Roadblock Removal
- Zero Tolerance
- Grading Performance

Continuous Improvement
- Standard Work
- Continuous Improvement
- Takt Control

As you can see this first book covers fewer points because the content is much more extensive. We will first tackle the topic of how to build high performance teams that are healthy and balanced. We will then discuss the principles that make up high performance senior superintendents who lead extraordinary teams. We will conclude with helpful guides and checklists to help you in your role.

This will be remarkable. As you read, please think of possible additions, stories, and feedback that can elevate this work. If you provide feedback, I will add you to the list of contributors in the book. So, let's first begin with...

THE ART OF THE BUILDER

The Captain

The cover of my previous book was an intentional image of a builder's head wearing a hard hat in the center of a construction site. The builder in the center was representative of a leader and all the things that a builder must control, including conditions, cleanliness, safety, organization, morale, culture and more. The project is a reflection of everything the builder has in their mind. The builder and the project are synonymous. If the builder is clean, the project will be clean. If the builder is on time, the project will be on time. If the builder is safe, then the project will be safe. The project is simply the physical manifestation of its builder's thoughts. The cover of this book is meant to communicate the need for multiple leaders to cohesively execute a project's logistics, strategies, and tactics. As a builder, you get to improve with the team to build remarkable projects. As a senior builder (a general), you must build people who can build projects as well as you can.

Based on one of my favorite book titles, *It's Your Ship: Management Techniques from the Best Damn Ship in the Navy* by Captain D. Michael Abrashoff for the purpose of this book, please imagine your project is a ship with you as captain. You are at the helm leading all other positions on your ship. You cannot operate the ship alone, and you cannot possibly lead at every level of operation. You must captain the ship which means you must lead the crew.

It's Your Ship is not only nicely written, it has energy and enthusiasm that can easily be applied to construction. As a lead superintendent I often referenced the military relation to construction. The sayings "Keep the ship in order. Keep the ship in orbit. Keep the ship afloat," communicates that we, as leaders, must create an environment where we can be stable. There are a number of lessons that accompany this perception, but suffice it to say that our charge is to keep our own ship in orbit or to keep our ship afloat. If the ship goes down, we go down with it. Remember, it's your job, and it's your ship. Here are the key concepts that feed into this role:

1. Make sure teams are functional and working well - (Build the Team)
2. Make sure people are trained - (Create Capability and Capacity)
3. Keep the ship properly stocked - (Logistics)
4. Make sure systems are maintained - (Operations)
5. Know where you are going - (Strategic Planning)
6. Communicate so that everybody knows how to get where you are going - (Short-Interval Planning)
7. Keep the ship in orbit - (Project Controls)

Key 1 - Teams are Working - (Build the Team)

As captain, first make sure all functional and fractal teams are operating at a high level. Encourage your teams to utilize resources and operating systems, communicate well, and have good team health. Every team should be composed of the proper people in their proper roles. Team members must be in close enough proximity to each other and develop rapport and connections despite their various personalities. Teams must be sized and structured to scale communication in their functional area. They must communicate well and take part in appropriate huddles and meeting systems. Captain, it is your responsibility to ensure that every team throughout the project is functioning properly through modeling, mentoring and support.

I remember a project with three functional areas—the exterior, the interior, and the basement. As captain of the jobsite I spent time with each of those teams in their huddles, meeting systems, and operations to ensure each of the teams were high functioning. I realized that my role had less to do with delegating and running the meetings and more to do with training and ensuring good team health. The challenge in application as captain is to make sure that you have high-functioning fractal teams throughout the project and throughout any level or part of your ship.

Key 2 - People are Trained - (Create Capability and Capacity)

For the second key concept, ensure people on your project are trained. This might seem like something that should be a given but often in our industry we expect people to arrive at our project site well-trained and knowing what to do, especially if they are contractors and vendors paid to do their job. This cannot be your assumption as a senior leader and captain of your ship. Every captain or leader must make sure that every functional and fractal team is trained to perform tasks well and spend time training so they are ready to succeed at their work.

I once encountered a concrete crew with foremen in charge of columns, walls, and decks who were not performing well. The company wasn't in a position to train them in their roles, consequently I immediately scheduled a daily hour-long meeting before our normal huddle system so they could upskill their roles as foremen. As a result, the concrete finished within hours of its original target date because we were able to achieve production and deal with the very difficult site circumstances by properly training the crew.

The key point is we didn't rely on somebody else, we didn't complain, we didn't yell, and we didn't send notices. We understood it was our job to train the crew members (within reason) and do what was required on the project.

Another time I was wholeheartedly attempting to implement Lean practices and principles on a construction project but the trade partners were not rising to the occasion. We immediately gave all the foremen a book-reading assignment and a 90-minute Lean training which ended up being a total of six hours of facilitated training. We did it so they could understand and implement Lean concepts on the project site - and It worked with great results. It is your job to make sure that everybody on your project site is well-trained for their role even if time is running short.

Sidenote: If you have a high-profile project with a high-profile owner, you can make requirements such as having all workers be OSHA 10 trained and certified, all foremen and supervisors to be OSHA 30 trained and certified, and have additional training for their roles. In summary, it is your job as the project leader to make sure that everybody is doing something they have been trained for and are qualified for.

Key 3 - Keep the Ship Properly Stocked - (Logistics)

The third concept is to keep the ship stocked. If you have a functional ship, and the people, you must make sure it's stocked with the proper logistical items including food, water, supplies, clothing, and fuel for the ship to function. Your ship needs the tools and equipment to properly accomplish its function.

There is no captain, either in fiction, nonfiction or anywhere, who would attempt to lead their ship and proceed to neglect stocking that ship—except perhaps Jack Sparrow in *Pirates of the Caribbean*. Military generals don't do it and neither should you. You have 100% complete responsibility, accountability, and ownership to stock and ensure the restocking of your ship. This will always be true of project, senior, and general superintendents. Stocking the project with materials, equipment, and resources cannot be delegated to the project engineers, or anybody else on the project site. It cannot be delegated to trade partners or the owner if there are owner-financed and contractor-installed items. As the captain of the ship, you are ultimately responsible for all procurement (not contractor buyout) throughout the project, from start to finish and beyond.

When I began my role as a project superintendent, I realized how true this principle is. There was a general superintendent who constantly told me, "Jason, if we can get it here, we can build it." So, I put those concepts together and made a plan to improve my mindset. I decided not to leave my fate in the hands of somebody else. I framed the situation like this: my success is hinged on whether or not we can build it. Whether or not we can build it is hinged on whether or not it is procured. Whether or not procurement has occurred hinges upon whether or not somebody else does their job. This chain of events has led me to take more initiative in the destiny of the project and ensure procurement is successful.

The superintendent is in charge of the material procurement, the supply chains, and all logistical aspects of the project. Taking charge of procurement ensures the project can be built with flow. A good general will lead the weekly procurement meeting and support the rest of the team. They will sit down and map out all the supply chains and ensure that the team is pulling materials, information, equipment, and other logistical needs to where they are needed on the project at the right time at the right rhythm. This is one of the reasons the US Military is so successful in battle. They are masters of logistics. Too often in construction we assume someone else will do this for us. This is a mistake.

Key 4 - Maintain the Ship's Systems - (Operations)

The fourth key concept to consider, as captain, is system maintenance. On a ship, certain key systems have to function properly for the ship to stay afloat. Systems on a ship include disposal systems, sanitation systems, potable water, power, and more. Food service must be working to feed the people on the ship in addition to other examples. Examples of systems that must be functioning on a construction project are as follows:

1. Hoisting systems
2. Delivery systems
3. Procurement systems
4. Information request systems
5. Safety monitoring systems
6. Survey control systems
7. Inspection systems
8. Quality systems and more

The bottom line, a captain on a ship, a senior superintendent on a site will ensure all systems are working properly. I remember a superintendent that said to me once, "If the damn office could get things here on time I could build this thing." I was disappointed in this comment because a good superintendent cannot ignore the systems that bring different components of the project together. A superintendent is not just an onsite delivery and installation coordinator. He is a process coordinator. A good superintendent will have accountability for these processes and not use a failed process as an excuse for failure. He will manage it and fix it to support the project.

Key 5 - You Know Where You Are Going - (Strategic Planning)

The fifth key concept for a captain to know is where he is going. If your ship is stocked with functioning systems, well organized teams, and trained people, you now need to know where you're going and what you need to get there. What is your mission? What are your orders? What are you supposed to do? As captain you must know the answers to these questions to serve your purpose. It is the project, senior or general superintendent's job to know where the ship's speed, direction and purpose is, just as builders must know what we are building, when it has to be built, how it is going to be built, and what is important to the customer.

An important principle in Lean thinking is that every project should know the voice of the customer, what the customer has paid for, and what the customer wants. The customer's wants and needs should be communicated throughout all levels of the project just like the mission would be properly communicated with the crew throughout the ship. Your job as the senior superintendent is to communicate the direction clearly.

One of my projects had a vivarium in the basement which was covered with waterproofing, protection board, and dirt. It was in a very high risk area for quality and water intrusion. Above that deck would be a considerable amount of water and runoff from the building roof, and the waterproofing was crucial in preventing it from entering the vivarium. The basement had to be covered by 3'-0" of dirt for the site. A condition of satisfaction for the owner was that the waterproofing had to be best in class. Due to the owner's request, the schedule, and the critical nature of the work, we had to create a plan to inspect and double inspect the waterproofing when backfilling. We used a single well-trained crew and enough time to meet the milestone at a slow and even pace.

We accomplished this because we prepared the work and did the proper pre-planning. We knew where we were going and we knew how to get there and kept the deadline by being ahead of the work and working as a team. We created an on-site rally cry with all the workers, foremen, and project team so they not only understood the requirements for waterproofing, but knew that it was in the owner's top five things that needed to be completed with excellent execution. It was remarkable.

In construction, as the captain, if you know what you're doing, where you're going, and what the mission is, and you know how, where, what, why, and when you're going to build it, the question then follows: have you scaled that communication to the rest of the project team so everybody can see as a group, know as a group, and act as a group?

Also, please remember the ship's Captain is not starting from scratch. He is part of a continuum which, ideally, included a deep dive with the Owner to define the project's North Star, Vision, Mission, and CoS, that guided the design from the beginning. This is the execution phase and the Strategic Planning is for executing on what the previous teams have already understood. It is your job to pass this on.

Key 6 - Everyone Knows How to Get There - (Short-Interval Planning)

Once you know where you're going as a captain of your ship, the sixth concept is to make sure that everybody knows how to get to the destination. It's one thing to say we are going to travel to a destination, but it's quite another thing to plan and map out where we're going, what we're going to do, and how far we have to go every day in order to accomplish the mission. In construction, everybody on the project team needs to know on a daily basis how we're going to build the project free of defects and on time. This will be done together as a team.

As captain of your ship, mapping the journey manifests into short-interval scheduling, six-week make-ready look ahead plans, weekly work plans, day plans, and daily huddles. To do this appropriately, you will set targets and consult with your trade partners on the best way to get there. This takes considerable skill to rally a team with trust, collaboration, and commitment. Once you know how you are going to get there based on team planning, everybody should know the short-interval steps to get to the ultimate goal. This breaking the project into daily, weekly, and monthly mini-marches with the project foreman will help you track well towards completion. As the senior superintendent, it is your job to create and implement highly effective meetings, huddles, and communication systems that will enable the execution of the short-interval plans with the trade partners. Additionally, the system you implement should get as much information as possible all the way to the workers, laborers, and vendors on-site. The workers should know with exact clarity what winning looks like, they should see when they're not winning, and know what they can do to recover and to start winning if they see deviations.

Key 7 - Keep the Ship Afloat (Project Controls)

The last major key is to ensure your ship doesn't sink. You must be productively paranoid and routinely ask "What is or could be going wrong and where might it occur?" There has to be a certain amount of productive paranoia with everything. It is up to you to make sure your ship stays afloat. You must always be proactive and anticipate future problems forecasting inventory and stock levels. To do this on a project, you must check that your procurement systems are feeding the project, supply chains are operational, and crews are communicating what they require. You must ensure your teams are well-organized and high functioning. You must be able to anticipate when these systems are about to break down and when your teams might need training for upcoming phases of work or else risk fragmenting into dysfunction. By using productive paranoia, you will see far enough into the future that you can anticipate problems and enable the crew to get to the end destination on time in daily increments. You will really win with this when you can create an environment where everyone does this with you.

I love the movie *Titanic*, especially when they hit the iceberg. The fictional scene depicting this event begins with people on the lookout who don't have the mindset to focus on their duty. In the scene, the crew members arrogantly said they could smell ice, without doing anything about it. It wasn't until they actually laid eyes on the iceberg that they hurriedly rang the bell to signal the first mate to respond. Even though they turned the ship to the starboard side and reversed the engines in their panic, as you know, they sustained damage, put lives in peril, and the ship went down within a matter of hours. There are a few things that really caused this tragedy. The captain failed to stay vigilant in his main role of ensuring the ship did not hit an iceberg. He failed to stay vigilant in making sure the watchmen in the lookout had their binoculars. He wasn't vigilant in making sure safety systems were working. He wasn't vigilant in making sure the crew was properly trained. He wasn't vigilant in making sure they were in the right roles. He wasn't vigilant in making sure they had the right supplies. He wasn't vigilant in helping the crew meet their short-interval goal sailing that night on their way to the overall goal of getting to New York because he did not listen and gain their input. He knew there were icebergs, and he knew they were going too fast. He wasn't focusing on all of his tasks, and he wasn't captaining the ship. Ultimately, he wasn't focusing on keeping his ship afloat. Therefore, the ship sank.

Where would the passengers have preferred the captain to be? Doing his role, or acquiescing to politicians and wishful thinking? The certain answer for the people on the *Titanic* is that they would have wanted the captain at the helm steering away from icebergs and keeping the ship afloat and doing his job. So when you think about delegating important tasks, leaving your station, abdicating your role, or being busy with lower-level work, just remember that your people want you at the helm keeping the ship afloat and keeping them safe. It is your job to keep the ship afloat. So, let's talk about how you steer a ship. We start with key number 1-build the team with...

THE ART OF THE BUILDER

Part 1 - Team Balance and Health

One of the first responsibilities of a senior superintendent is to build the team. Remember, always focus on *who* then *what*. As Jim Collins says, "First, get the right people on the bus, the wrong people off, and then figure out where to drive it." Often the super has the opinion that the people on his jobsite are not his friends but there to do a job. This is a shame. While they may not be his "friends", they are people, and people need connection, relevance, and measurement to be fully engaged and productive. That is why a team must be balanced and healthy to be effective.

--Connection and relevance ensure a person on a team is healthy.
--Measurement and the ability to win makes a person on a team balanced.

To generate high productivity with people, a leader must create high levels of balance and health. Patrick Lencioni said, "A former client, the founder of a billion dollar company, best expressed the power of teamwork, when he once told me, 'If you could get all the people in the organization rowing in the same direction, you could dominate any industry in any market against any competition at any time.'" Whenever I repeat this adage to a group of leaders, they immediately nod their heads, but in a desperate sort of way. They seem to grasp the truth of it while simultaneously surrendering to the impossibility of actually making it happen. Here's how we address those dysfunctions. To begin improving your team and to better understand the level of dysfunction you're facing, ask yourself these simple team health questions:

- Do team members openly share their opinions in meetings and at other times?
- Are all team players engaged and willing to share?
- Are all team members regularly engaging in healthy conflict resolution on the team instead of holding back and gossiping at home or at work?
- Do team members hold each other accountable before you have to step in?
- Can the team come to decisions quickly and avoid getting bogged down?
- Do team members confront each other about their shortcomings?
- Do team members sacrifice their own interests for the good of the team?

If the answers to these questions are not all yes, then the good news is that you are like everyone else in this industry and have opportunities to improve. To start, let's work on...

Your Motive

Most of the content you will read in the following sections come from books written by Patrick Lencioni, founder of The Table Group. I recommend his book, *The Motive: Why So Many Leaders Abdicate Their Most Important Responsibilities* to any senior superintendent or project manager and to use it in assessing whether they are willing to do the things that leaders do. *Your Motive* is titled to introduce the question, What is your motive for being a leader? Is it to serve or be served? Let's see...

Every leader must do five key things to be successful and support team balance and health:

1. Build the team first.
2. Have hard conversations.
3. Manage, coach, and mentor direct reports.
4. Hold remarkable meetings.
5. Scale communication.

These may seem simple at first, but they are not. Any one of these five when truly implemented with proper expectations would make the best of us wonder if we wanted to be leaders. So, here we go...

1. Build the team first. Every leader gets to do the things that no one can do or will do. Building the team is one of those things. People are irrational, illogical, and emotional human beings with varying communication styles. Building teams is a messy thing. Also, it is something you have to constantly work at, because once you peel the layer off the onion of team development, another layer lies beneath. But the senior superintendent will rise up to this challenge and spend more time with people than with tasks. I remember a general superintendent at Hensel Phelps telling me, "Jason, I spend most or all of my time with the people on this team. I go from person to person ensuring they have the training and resources to do their job well." That has always stuck with me. To be effective, your team needs a team builder before they need a taskmaster and worker.

2. Have hard conversations. Teams must be managed. New age concepts of hiring the right person and leaving them alone to do their work are not only impractical, they are irresponsible. You will actually do more harm to someone if you leave them alone

rather than be their manager and leader, even with newer generations. Growth is hard, and leaders get to say the hard things. But, saying hard things doesn't mean the manager has to say it in a hard way. If a direct report or person on the team needs correction, feedback, or cajoling, the leader must give it. If there is a difficult situation to solve, the leader gets to solve it. Yes, I said, "get to." That's because you chose to be a leader and that means you must also choose to say the hard things. I remember a prominent leader saying, "those who do not say what needs to be said for fear of offending someone are only thinking of themselves." We as leaders must put our people first. If we do not say the hard things, we are only temporarily comforting ourselves while abdicating our responsibility.

3. Manage, coach, and mentor direct reports. As a leader it is your job to train the team. This cannot be abdicated! There should never be a time when you arrive at a project and assume that the team is "trained" in their responsibilities. They are NOT! You will be better off to assume previous leaders may have abdicated their responsibilities when it comes to your team. No one is ever done being trained or done learning for themselves. As a project leader you must manage, coach, and mentor direct reports. It is like being the coach of a football team. No good coach would ever take over a team and assume every player is already performing at a high level. A coach would immediately set in to manage the team, coach the players, and mentor those who needed it.

4. Hold remarkable meetings. Leaders do not allow mediocre meetings. If there are garbage meetings on a project you supervise, you are not being a

leader. Ineffective meetings waste too much time and energy and become detrimental to the success of a project. All meetings, from the OAC to the team meeting and all the way to worker huddles, should be focused, relevant, and interesting. If not, you are wasting the most valuable resource on the project—team capacity and energy. A great leader must ensure all meetings are run in a remarkable way. On a project site, meetings are the main system of communication, so they must operate well for the team to succeed. If you want certain defeat, muzzle your communications by holding useless meetings.

5. Scale communication. Leaders repeat things a minimum of seven times. The clarity of where the project is headed, why it is headed there, and how it will arrive there should be made perfectly clear to everyone on the project site. Once a leader feels like they are clearly communicating the vision of the project, multiply that tenfold and understand it is just the beginning. Leaders repeat things ad nauseum. Once every worker on the project can repeat by memory the customer's top needs, the end date, and the plan for the day, that is when the communication goal has been accomplished. I can promise you we are not there yet.

Once promoted, some leaders feel like they have "arrived" in their position and can sit back and enjoy their cushy chair while others do the work. The exact opposite of that is true. Once a leader arrives at their position, they now get to do the gut-wrenching and horrific work of managing difficult people situations and the wonderful work of building teams. They get to do what others can't do and won't do. As stated before, if a leader does not do those five things, or is unwilling to do them, he or she is not a leader and should step down.

The Five Behaviors

Once we have the right motive on our journey of building the team, we can turn our attention to what makes teams great. To introduce this topic, let me first explain what a team is by referencing the book, *The Wisdom of Teams: Creating the High-Performance Organization* by Jon R. Katzenbach and Douglas K. Smith.

The Team Performance Curve:

Working Group: This is a group for which there is no significant incremental performance need or opportunity that would require it to become a team. The members interact primarily to share information, best practices, or perspectives and to make decisions to help each individual perform within his or her area of responsibility.

Pseudo Team: This is a group for which there could be a significant, incremental performance need or opportunity, but it **has not focused on collective performance and is not really trying to achieve it.** It has no interest in shaping a common purpose or set of performance goals, even though it may call itself a team. Pseudo teams are the weakest of all groups in terms of performance impact.

Potential Team: This is a group for which there is a significant, incremental performance need that is really trying to improve its performance impact. However, it typically requires more clarity about purpose, goals or work-products and more discipline in hammering out a common working approach. **It has not yet established collective accountability.**

Real Team: This is a small number of people with complementary skills who are equally committed to a common purpose, goals, and working approach for which they **hold themselves mutually accountable.**

High Performance Team: This is a group that meets all the conditions of real teams and has members who are also deeply committed to each other's personal growth and success. That commitment usually transcends the team. The high performance team significantly outperforms all other like teams and outperforms all reasonable expectations given its membership.

I hope you found those definitions from *The Wisdom of Teams* helpful. I have bolded the sections that are particularly important to me in the definitions. What was the common theme among the definitions? I hope at least a part of your answer was "accountability." If it was, you are on to the secret of building teams—mutual accountability. This leads us to the five key behaviors of a team. They are trust, healthy conflict, goal setting, accountability and performing. Have you ever been on an underperforming team that lacked accountability? If so, it is likely the team didn't set standards and goals together nor did they engage in healthy conflict and share their opinions. They likely didn't share their opinions because they didn't trust each other because they didn't know each other. Lastly, they never made it through these behavior stages because there wasn't a multiplier leader to lead them through the target behaviors toward a strenuous performance goal. We will discuss the multiplier leader in just a bit, but first, let's dive deep into the five behaviors. We will start with…

Behavior 1 - Trust

An absence of trust happens when team members are reluctant to be vulnerable with one another and are unwilling to admit their mistakes, weaknesses, or needs for help. Without a certain comfort level among team members, a foundation for trust is impossible. One time, when I was working in my home office, my partner and wife, Kate, asked if I had seen a certain video by Simon Sinek about trust. I ignored it at first but was later prompted to take it seriously and watch it. I'm glad I did. In the video, Sinek explained how he interviewed Navy SEAL instructors about how they staffed SEAL Team Six, the most famous and high-performing SEAL team. They explained it to him like this: There are really two measurable scales in this instance—performance and trust. Someone could be scaled from high performance to low performance and high trust to low trust. The instructors told Sinek they would rather staff their highest performing seal team with someone that was medium performance and high trust before someone that was high performance but low trust. Because they follow that model, they are always able to staff SEAL Team Six with the right people. That little story is interesting—a medium performer that can be highly trusted is more valuable to an organization than a high performer with low trust. Let's see why...

If there is no trust, there is no willingness to engage in healthy conflict, a topic we will cover in the next section. A construction project cannot succeed with one person calling all the shots. Projects are too big, too complex, and too fast-paced to do them alone. You need a high performing team with high standards and one that holds each other mutually accountable. Without trust, there can be no accountability because there is no open communication. People will not open up and talk about real things if they do not trust each other. No team will ever progress if they neglect to build trust.

People begin building trust when they know each other. In Stephen M.R. Covey's book, *Leading at the Speed of Trust*, he lists three key things that are crucial to building trust:

1. Intentions
2. Track Record
3. Experience

Basically, to trust someone you must know their intentions, track record, history of performance, and depth of experience within their role. A group of people must build trust so they can truly communicate to become a team. They can only build trust if they know each other, have proximity, create connections and build rapport. The kicker is...none of this is possible without transparency.

Transparency manifests itself in many different ways but to summarize, in order for a person to build trust they must:

1. Share what they think and feel.
2. Be honest and have integrity in all they do.
3. Be open, approachable, and present with other members of the team.
4. Share and make decisions with the team in a transparent way.
5. Be vulnerable and open with the team emotionally. This means expressing when they have been offended and apologizing when they have offended someone else.

If these are not in place, there will be no trust.

So, how do we create transparency you ask. I have listed below some techniques which can be used to create a transparent environment and build trust:

Transparency Techniques:

- Copy everyone on your team on emails, Important team texts, and meetings-
    - Don't freak out on me just yet. A high performing team will pare this down after a while, but at first, and maybe even the first few months, the team should copy each other on every email including critical team texts or messages, and loop other

team members into most meetings, even if it is only as an optional attendee. After the initial period, the team will learn what things do not need to be shared; but the starting default should be EVERYTHING! Obviously "reply to all' thank you emails are a waste of time. As the team gets more comfortable and disciplined, they will learn to be more specific and intentional about who they copy. This is one of the most important things you can do on your team to build transparency and trust.

- Share calendars
    - Sharing calendars is similar to copying people on emails. I remember as a superintendent not wanting to share my calendar or copy people on emails. I remember moments where I wanted to make a decision in a silo, spend money with no accountability, fire off that nasty email without a second set of eyes, attend that meeting alone so I could have ultimate control; I can say it was never worth it. As I disciplined myself to share and be open, I made better decisions, had more support, and performed better as a leader. Share your calendar with your team. You have nothing to hide and the alignment you will get from it will only make you better.

- Share personal goals
    - One of the best things a team can do is create player cards. Player cards are cards of summarized information from an individual survey and personality profiles. They are conversation starters. A well-crafted player card builds rapport and tailors safe communication for each person

individually. In fact, I like the player cards so much I recommend posting these at each team member's desk for team members to get to know each other. It is powerful for a team to know where each member is currently. Consider also how powerful it could be if the team also knew where the person was going. I like to post a player card incorporating a person's goals near their desk. These goals do not have to be too personal, and should be appropriate to share openly.

There was a project where I posted my goals pertaining to how I could better address feedback for improvement. I can honestly say that every other member of the team helped me reach those goals, and that was around the same time my career began to skyrocket. It was so successful we all shared and posted our player cards with our goals. Because they were seen by the entire team, the entire team helped each other achieve their individual goals. This is one of my favorite practices to build trust among a team. How can you not like someone or build rapport when they know you and are helping you reach your goals? The answer is obvious.

- Close doors only when necessary
    - I have an analogy about closed office doors. For this, let's use the old shoulder devil and angel characters on Looney Tunes and Disney cartoons. If the devil wanted to cause ruin and despair to a construction team the first thing he would do is build walls throughout the office. Once that was done, he would encourage siloed communication systems, close-doored

meetings, suspicion, toxic hierarchy and watch the team fall apart while the project crash lands. Nothing will ruin a good team faster than doors and walls. Even though open office spaces can be a bit noisy and annoying, they are healthy for the team. The shared space creates trust, transparency and collaboration, which gives way to a common team culture generating a fun and dynamic environment.

- When people are locked away in ivory towers, they tend to favor siloed thinking, minimal communication, and individual productivity over teaming. Remember the goal of a team is to work together and increase communication, as well as individual productivity. Here is the best part. You can have individual productivity, proximity, trust, and collaboration with an open office that also has break-out rooms, production pods, and a quality pair of noise canceling headphones. Your team should be out in the open, working, and communicating together. It's ultimately up to you, but please trust me on this… Soloed offices hurt collaborative cultures.

- Do not play boss

    - In an over hierarchical environment trust and transparency are reduced. Unfortunately there will always be hierarchy in construction, but that hierarchy should not be flaunted or punctuated. If you continually begin sentences that start with "I am going to have you…" or "You will do…" or "I am your boss…," then you are undermining and reducing the team's psychological safety in that situation. Your direct report is likely only thinking, "What should I say or do or be so that I can avoid getting in trouble and impress my boss?" When the leader inverts the hierarchy pyramid, making leadership about serving and focusing on reducing roadblocks, the leader can then get everyone on the boat, in the right seat, point out the end goal, and say "let's get rowing together".

- Be a go-giver
    - And finally, the secret to any relationship is to give to the other person; be the go-giver. I remember fighting constantly with a PM on one of my projects. The PM and I did not see eye to eye and it was affecting the team. I read the book *The Go-giver* by Bob Burg and John David Mann, and began to practice thinking about the PM's needs more than what I needed from him. This sounds like a corny cat poster or love story, but I can tell you he and I became great friends and coworkers. We shared more, made better decisions together and to this day, he is still my favorite PM to work with. Expansion of this idea works with companies, teams, individuals, team members and anyone who is interested in building trust and transparency. How can you not be transparent with someone who is giving to you? You are naturally wired to connect with them when it happens. If you want to build trust and create transparency, give!

What items would you add to the list to create trust? Here are some ideas for you as you think about this question:

- Be yourself.
- Be vulnerable.

- Show integrity: Do what you say you are going to do.
- Talk straight.
- Demonstrate respect.
- Show loyalty.
- Right wrongs.
- Deliver results.
- Be coachable and always look to get better.
- Confront the true reality.
- Listen first.
- Clarify expectations.
- Take responsibility.
- Keep commitments.
- Extend trust to others.
- Create trustworthiness with the small things.

In conclusion, transparency builds trust because people trust what they can see, understand and align with. If you want to build trust, create transparent environments. Stephen M. R. Covey said, "Without trust we don't truly collaborate, we merely coordinate or at best cooperate. It is trust that transforms a group of people into a team." It is your decision to create an environment full of trust and transparency. What will you do? Because only after you have built trust can you engage in...

Behavior 2 - Healthy Conflict

Second, fear of conflict. Teams lacking in trust are incapable of engaging in unfiltered, passionate debate about key issues. A lack of debate causes situations where team conflict can easily turn into veiled discussions and back channel comments. In a work setting where team members do not openly air their opinions, inferior decisions and buy-in are the result. If people won't speak up about the truth, that's where evil is hidden, where problems fester and where we stop protecting the innocent. We must stay diligent and communicate with courage via radical but compassionate candor .

Let me tell you a story about my journey with healthy conflict. I remember going into a team meeting on my project and saying, "Hey, let's all read this book about the Five Dysfunctions of a Team." Honestly, I thought reading this book would magically fix our team dynamics just by having people read it. After about two weeks I asked, "Hey, did everybody read that book? Alright, let's talk about it. Let's do something." To break the silence that followed I said, "Yeah, but you know, hey, we know this model, we can start working through this. Let's start building trust. Let's start having healthy conflict. Let's start doing this." More crickets. And so I did what any ignorant 33 year-old super would do, I began practicing these concepts alone. I got all trashy. I was like, "Woo-hoo, I've got a license to start engaging in conflict around here." So I became kind of a problem for a little bit. I just told everybody what I thought, and it went in the wrong direction. I finally realized I was way off when I went to Lean Congress in 2017 and I heard concepts that were presented by Patrick Lencioni, and I was able to wake up.

Using his right and left hands, Patrick showed his audience. "If this is no conflict...and if this is hell...you want to be somewhere in the middle, you want to start inching people towards that middle." As he moved his hand in little increments, I had a sudden and clear insight. "Ooh, I got that wrong. I need to go back, re-frame and fix things." I realized that in getting past the five dysfunctions of a team, there's a process there, and it is very intentional, and we really, really have to work at it in a specific way. When I returned to the job, we intentionally started working at it the right way. We used his exercises and took the advice from his book. We asked the team, "How can we build trust? What kind of healthy conflict can we engage in so that we can get to more of the ideal? How do you like feedback according to your personality type?" With that trust and willingness to engage in healthy conflict, we facilitated goal teaming sessions and asked, "What are we trying to do this month? This week? This next phase of the project?" and we made better decisions together. It was remarkable.

For the people out there who have built their careers being politically correct and never engage in these behaviors, never speak up, and never try to get out of this false harmony mode, I want to say: You will never, never, never, never, never, never, never, never, ever build a team unless you're willing to have healthy conflict and hold each other accountable. In order to prioritize the needs of the team, we need to gather our courage, and be willing, brave and courageous enough to speak up, to step up, and to go get it done. There are two different scenarios that we're dealing with, and I do want to be clear one more time. In life in general, one-on-one, the book *How to Win Friends and Influence People* by Dale Carnegie, my favorite book on earth, will be your guiding star that will guide you most of the time. The crowning advice in that book is that the only way you can win an argument is to avoid it. That is true, but is only applicable in life outside of the realm of a team.

In team building, you have to have "healthy" conflict mode. Which is "speak up" mode. And, "hey, I'm gonna talk, I'm gonna hold people accountable, I'm gonna raise my hand, I'm gonna say uncomfortable things," mode. When we need to build a team, we need to speak up. Fear of conflict allows teams to fail, and should be avoided at most costs. There are safe ways to communicate and engage in healthy conflict. After all, we have personality profiles that tell us how people want feedback. If you find safe pathways to communicate then you can make sure there is no unhealthy conflict and bring all comments to the healthy side of the spectrum. To help, I have listed some things to remember in your healthy conflict plan.

- Anger is fear - Remember, anger is fear-based and should not be a motivator to speak up with the team. Any coward can speak up when they are attacked or angry. Only the brave can do it calmly.

- Controlling behavior is unhealthy - Do not confuse healthy conflict with controlling behavior. When you bring something up as healthy conflict, it must be to move the team forward, not to gain control.

- No one will like conflict - Remember that no one really likes conflict so it must be practiced. Also, very few are naturally good at it so it must be practiced by everyone. The clinical answer for how to get better with this is practice, practice, and practice some more. Remember, practice makes permanent.

- There is an unhealthy side - We have to remember that there is a spectrum. On one side is false harmony and the other side is hell. We want to be in the middle. When a team member steps too far onto the hell side, it is important for a team member or leader to call that out and inch the team back to the middle.

- Remove hierarchy - If you are going to coach people to speak up, they must feel as little hierarchy in that space as possible. People will speak up more when they feel they have the freedom to do so.

- Accountability does not work outside of a team - Remember that having healthy conflict with just anybody may not work. I am encouraging you to engage in healthy conflict within your core group where it is expected and practiced. Remember, you may get into a bit of trouble if you practice this concept with just anyone.

In summary, you must be able to engage in healthy conflict to make better decisions, standards, and goals. If you will not, you will never have an aligned team. If you do not, you will never improve as a team. If you do not, you will never harness the power of the team. The best teams speak up and hold each other mutually accountable. But accountability only happens when the team starts…

Behavior 3 - Setting Goals and Standards Together

I remember a time when I was teaching my family about these concepts. My daughter Effie told my son Reno to take off his hat during family prayer. As you might expect my son replied, "Effie, my darling sister, I am so happy you said something. I really appreciate that reminder." JUST KIDDING! He did not say that. We are real people over here. What he said was "Stop bossing me around Effie!" and then they began to argue. In this instance I could not come to the aid of daddy's little girl because "taking hats off during prayer" is not something we had discussed as a family (team) and set as a standard. I told Effie, "If you are simply telling him to do something because you want it done, that is called being controlling. If you are holding him accountable to a team standard, that is called being a team member." She understood and it has not been an issue since that time. We know as a family that we only hold each other accountable for agreed-upon or commonly known standards. The same concept holds true for a project team. There must be commonly agreed upon standards and goals to hold someone accountable.

The project team should be intentional about creating and communicating standards for the team to follow in the path to be excellent.

Here are some examples of things that should be clear with full buy-in from the team:

- How each person wants interaction on the team
- Project success goals
- Key performance indicators to measure project success
- Team behaviors and culture
- Safety rules and enforcement methods
- The quality plan
- Internal and external communication systems
- Project Management system procedures
- Expectations for trade partners and vendors
- Site zero tolerance rules

I will give two examples to show what I mean. The first one is from the "This Is Me," template I use on projects. It's a survey that helps create safe pathways for communication. I use these to build the team and ultimately to transfer key information onto a person's player card. The second example is a list of team behaviors for a project. I hope you enjoy them.

"This Is Me" Questions:
- What are the types of communication that help you the most with your team: (Explain)
- You try to be easy to get along with, but like most people you have a few "hot buttons." Very briefly, what are they? (Explain)

- What is your biggest strength?
- How can we encourage you in your strengths?
- What is your biggest weakness?
- How can we help you overcome your weakness?
- How do you like interaction when you have reached a point of stress?
- When a team member has identified a potential blind spot in your role, how would you like feedback?
- What is one thing you want us to know?

Answers to these questions can lead a team to engage in healthy conflict safely and set a standard for communication between team members. This tool takes communicating from assumption to standard. After answering these questions, there is no ambiguity about how we communicate. Now, we can hold each other accountable to it.

Project Team Behaviors:

Behaviors -
- Give first. Help others in their role.
- Bring problems to the surface.
- Widen your circle when problems arise.
- Decide as a majority, act in unison as a team
- Mine for conflict in every meeting.
- No "end-rounding." Weigh in and buy in for all decisions.
- Fanatically find and remove roadblocks daily.
- Take time to train and develop each other.

Beliefs -
- The problem is not that there are problems. The problem is expecting otherwise and thinking having problems is a problem. Bring all problems to the surface
- There is no such thing as one person's problem. All problems belong to the team.
- Nothing good thrives in secrecy or a lack of accountability. Only at the surface, in the daylight, and amongst the team can anything healthy thrive.
- The goal of project leaders is to provide clarity behind expectations, how the expectations meet project goals, and how each team member adds value in that framework. Leaders must stay at the helm and provide clarity as their first priority.
- The project only succeeds when it is under budget, on time, done safely, with quality, the team health is good, and people meet their career goals with a raving fan customer

As you can see in this example, certain behaviors and beliefs are clear and agreed upon by the team. Now any member of the team can hold any other member accountable for their part in these. That is when things get remarkable. This allows the team to really practice...

Behavior 4 - Accountability

Accountability is the last real behavior in team development. As I said before, once the team has trust, engages in healthy conflict, & sets goals and standards together, they can hold each other accountable to those standards. Although this behavior needs the first three, this one is the most important. A potential team will never become a team until they hold each other mutually accountable.

At Elevate Construction, we are able to host dozens of immersive boot camps for workers, foremen, field engineers, and superintendents every year. The process for these camps are very real and very effective. As an example, I will mention the granddaddy of all boot camps—the field engineer boot camp. This is a seven-day camp where participants actually research, draft, lay out, and build a real structure. They have four days to do it, and they must do it as a team, sometimes working between 14 and 17 hours a day to complete the assignment. The main ingredient for the winning team is accountability. Our instructors constantly praise participants when the team begins to hold itself accountable. Up until that point the team members silo, get distracted, break down, and start fighting. The team members get demoralized, and are unable to solve problems quickly enough to make a schedule. As teams near the breaking point, they usually realize they should heed our advice and hold each other accountable.

Eventually one team member reminds the team to collaborate. Another goes over to help someone with a CAD problem. The leader checks a set of field notes someone else has written. A team member starts to call out another person with a bad attitude, and it snowballs from there. They begin to realize they are only going to make it through this camp if they begin to help each other, and that help comes in the form of support and—most importantly—accountability for what the team is doing, how they will do it, and when it needs to get done. This is when the team really performs. Teams that do not get through the "Rumble" to this point do not finish on time. The other accountability-centered teams have to step in and pull the non-accountable teams across the finish line. It is a sight to see.

This scenario plays out in each of our lives every day. We are mediocre at home, at work, at church, and with ourselves until we get a good dose of accountability from someone else or ourselves. I can't really explain it any better than that. And, as I am writing this, I fear you still don't realize the full depth of what I am saying, and although it would be my fault if this were the case, I cannot help but lament the thought that you would leave this section without feeling in your heart and mind that all success in a team comes from accountability. This accountability allows the team to focus on...

Behavior 5 - Performance

If a team has lost sight of the necessity of achievement, the project ultimately suffers. Everyone reading this has seen teams that are not performing because they will not hold each other mutually accountable. A team lacks accountability because they will not set goals and standards together. They will not set goals and standards together because they will not engage in healthy conflict. They don't engage in healthy conflict because they do not trust each other, and they do not trust each other because they are not transparent and do not know each other. So here and now we have the formula, the pattern, and the model. If we want to perform and win as a team, this is the way.

It is important to know this because I have only ever seen a team take a turn for positive change if one of the following things happen:

1. A catastrophe occurs. A death on a project or a major accident wakes a project up and the team begins acting like a team.
2. The team is removed, reorganized, or replaced.
3. A leader comes in and drives the team. The leader is smart enough to make decisions that direct the team to a higher performance.
4. The team learns about these principles and intentionally implements them together according to the model. I would prefer this fourth option for you.

Which one of these is the most sustainable? The answer is obvious. I invite you to read Patrick Lencioni's book, *The Five Dysfunctions of a Team: A Leadership Fable*, and use these five behaviors on your project.

The Big Three - Team Development

I have been privileged to help recover many teams in my career. While the five behaviors have been crucial in my efforts, there are two other considerations that must be evaluated when assessing a team—the leader and the goal. The five behaviors only work if there is a multiplier leader supporting their team and a strenuous performance goal magnetizing the team towards higher performance. If a team is struggling, One of the following three things are missing: the five behaviors, the multiplier leader, or the goal. So, let's start with the...

Multiplier Leader

There are multiplier leaders and diminishing leaders. Every great team needs a multiplier leader to support the functions of the team. Let's dive right into this concept.

Diminishers:

Diminishing leaders argue their people are overworked and the best people are maxed out, therefore, accomplishing a bigger task requires the addition of more resources. That logic might seem persuasive, logical, and reasonable, but that's the logic of addition.

We should be following the logic of opportunity which means that we should have a multiplication belief. Multipliers understand that most people in organizations are under-utilized, and unused capability can be leveraged with the right kind of leadership. Therefore, institutional intelligence and capability can be multiplied without requiring a bigger investment.

Have you ever been around somebody who sucks the energy out of the room, who micromanages you, or swoops in and saves you and takes assignments over? If so, you are working with a diminisher. You likely feel you are working for them, you're not at 100% utilization or engagement, and you feel limited. You feel like you're handcuffed, like they will step into lower level tasks and take over for you. You are being diminished in your role.

These leaders are absorbed in their own intelligence, stifle others, and deplete the organization of crucial intelligence and capability because they believe intelligence is based on elitism and scarcity. They think they are smarter than other people or they feel like intelligent people are a rare breed. They feel intelligence is not common, people can't be taught, and people aren't naturally brilliant.

Diminisher Leaders:
1. Believe people cannot figure things out without them.
2. Hire people to underutilize them and lord over them.
3. Hoard resources.
4. Create tense environments.
5. Use fear and anxiety to motivate people.
6. Make all the decisions.
7. Micromanage people, playing savior with the team.

I once worked with a diminishing leader. Almost every current effort at the company was stalled at his inbox. He did not want people moving forward without him and he did not know how to organize his time or be responsible with communication, so nothing ever got past his inbox, his messages, or your conversation with him. He would always blame the roadblock on someone else and blame the direct report for, "Not getting his attention." In my role I had a mission, a directive, and all the makings of a good team with my groups, but I had someone over me that was diminishing my efforts. And just so you don't think I was being a victim in that circumstance, I will happily report that I eventually quit. Once I was out of his diminishing environment, I went on to accomplish a unimaginable amount of things.

Multipliers:

Multipliers enable their team to feel trusted and coached in a very progressive and dynamic way. Their team loves coming to work because the multiplier invests time and energy into their success. The team feels supported because the multiplier holds their people up in tough times. Multipliers are genius makers; as author Jim Collins said, "they're not time tellers, they're clock builders." Multipliers actually work through people, build the collective intelligence of the team, and believe that intelligence is continually developing.

They believe people are smart and can figure things out through proper coaching and management. They know their organization is full of talented people and they just need to find them. Instead of writing people off as not worth their time, they ask what can be done to develop and grow their capabilities. They provide training, believe in professional development, and believe their job is to bring the right people together in an environment that liberates people's best thinking.

Multipliers:
1. Believe people are smart.
2. Hire talented people.
3. Help people succeed.
4. Create intense environments that challenge people to perform.

5. Encourage healthy conflict, and,
6. Invest time in people.

I was able to work for a multiplier once. He gave me a clear vision, mission, and the support to carry it out. He was one of the best leaders I ever worked with. I remember a time when I was placed in charge of a highly important task in the midst of hundreds of employees on a single project. I put together the plan with a team, refined it, and prepared to present to the superintendent group. When I arrived in the meeting and began to present, I was met with a host of criticisms and skeptical comments. My leader spoke up in the middle of this and said, "Hey, I am fine for you to give him feedback, but the best thing to do is to let Schroeder do what he does." His message was to trust the plan and the individual, and to have a responsible, not critical, review of it. When I heard that comment I wanted to work doubly hard, because I knew he trusted me. He had effectively multiplied my efforts and motivation.

Diminishers say, "They will never figure this out without me" while multipliers say, "People are smart and we'll figure this out through good coaching." Diminishers use talent while multipliers develop talent. Diminishers blame people while multipliers explore and learn from the situation. If you see a leader saying, "Well, they didn't do much with that" or, "they are to blame," or, "they messed that up" instead of looking at how they could have corrected or aided with the process or the situation, you'll know that you're talking to a diminisher versus a multiplier.

In order to properly build the team, we need a multiplier leader at the helm. This is important to the system because a team needs a facilitator who will allow and enable others to be high performers on the team. A diminisher will never get this done and will hurt the team more than help it. So while learning the five behaviors is great, they will do us no good without a multiplier leader to create engagement and support for the team entering into those behaviors. I recommend reading *Multipliers: How the Best Leaders Make Everyone Smarter* by Liz Wiseman. That leads us into having a…

Strenuous Performance Goal

To really come together as a team, a group needs a performance challenge. A high-performing team must have a clear, specific purpose that is distinct and aligned with the purpose of the larger organization. The team has to have a hill to climb, an army to conquer, or a mission to complete-a 20-mile march if you will. There has to be a real need that pulls everyone up, magnetizes everybody, and creates momentum.

I once worked with a company that wanted to improve field operations. We focused first on optimizing their pre-construction efforts. After months of implementation, the company was starting all projects with a Takt plan, constructability review, a fully developed project plan, and a "fresh eyes" meeting ahead of the project start to ensure the plan was complete. We felt the teams had everything needed at that point but I was surprised to see a few teams stumble right out of the gate when beginning the project. It was a very large two hundred and forty million dollar project where the team allowed things to get eight weeks behind schedule. The owner was not happy and I was alarmed. Upon investigating, I found the team had grown complacent. Because they were so set up and well prepared they believed they could not fail. But they did fail. What they needed was a goal, an emergency, a milestone. I mentioned this to the team and they immediately picked a milestone for their mat foundations. The team rallied, drove through the four phases of team development, and started getting the time back. After that first milestone setting, the team always had a strenuous performance goal to track to.

And they finished the project on time, under budget, and with a raving fan customer.

To really win, every team needs a strenuous performance goal in addition to a multiplier leader. To learn more about creating a strenuous performance goal, please consider reading *Silos, Politics, and Turf Wars* by Patrick Lencioni. Install a multiplier leader, set strenuous performance goals, build the team through the five behaviors and then watch as that team rises to the occasion. It is a remarkable process. At this point I have referenced the phases of team development twice. It may be a good point to tackle...

The Phases of Team Development

The phases of team development describe how teams behave and what to expect as they are coming together. The four phases are Forming, Storming, Norming, and Performing.

First, Forming the team. As a group comes together, it is really a potential team that can become something more. Group members may have a lot of questions about what to expect and who to expect it from. There is usually more excitement than conflict in this phase because individuals may still be excited about the opportunity and possibilities. This is the phase when members will ask for and want more direction, clarity, and an understanding of their roles. The first immediate step is to get people to understand each other. Building trust must come ahead of the Storming phase. Creating standard meeting systems, increasing proximity, getting to know each other, and implementing transparency techniques are crucial here. I like to draw this phase with arrows pointing to a center to emphasize a group coming together.

Second, Storming. The team will begin stepping on each other's toes. Conflict is inevitable with a developing team.

There will be a misalignment of communication styles, people performing out of their roles, and a host of things will create conflict. Some of this will be healthy and some will be unhealthy. The key here is to let it happen and steer it towards the middle of the false harmony and hell spectrum. This is a little like being on a National Geographic field shoot. You just need to stand back and let nature happen unless you see abusive behavior or something that has crossed a line. Do not restrain the team too much or they will stop speaking up. Most people were taught to shut up and sit down in school; we, as the leaders, cannot let the team get to that mode which is unhealthy behavior. The key is to praise the team for speaking up, encourage them to know when they are being falsely harmonious, and if necessary steer them back if they have gone too far to the hell side of the spectrum. Your team will never develop if you do not lead them through the storming phase. There is no going around it.

Third, Norming. At this point potential team members might have hit a groove where they normalize their work, their role, and their interactions with each other. This is desired because people need to spend time in their comfort, fear, learning, and growth zones at different times in their life. They cannot spend too much time in any one of them. At this point the leader is crucial to the success of the potential team. Members will rally within their roles and leaders should be focusing on higher levels of performance. This is a great step forward. By this time the team should have proximity, working communication systems, meeting systems, personality profiles, scorecards for their roles, and more overall organization to the team. This is the point when the team needs to begin creating standards and goals. The team can then use their ability to engage in healthy conflict, and hold each other accountable. At this point the leader needs to encourage conflict in every meeting and reinforce how accountability works within the team. As they begin to normalize, they will transition to...

The last step, Performing. In the performing team, the leader is among the team, not the central figurehead. The team is working; it has a clear performance goal becoming the galvanizing aspect that the team drives toward. In this step we should see people speaking up, clarifying goals and expectations, and holding each other mutually accountable. The team will feel like a team, a well oiled machine. To become a high performance team, each member must take a personal interest in the goals and the well-being of the other members. You will see this type of team doing a lot of giving, spending time with each other, and being vulnerable. This is where we want our teams to be. It is not easy, but it is possible.

The list that follows will help you through the phases of team development. Make sure to focus on the steps listed in each phase to keep up your momentum:

Forming:
- Clearly identify roles.
- Perform personality profiles to get to know each other.
- Begin building safe pathways for communication.

Storming:
- Encourage healthy conflict.
- Mine for conflict in meetings.
- Build trust by increasing proximity and rapport.
- Increase transparency and vulnerability.

Norming:
- Normalize good meetings.
- Normalize communication systems.

- Implement team coverage systems.
- Begin grading team health.
- Acknowledge that the leader is the central figure.

Performing:
- Celebrate wins.
- Reward the team.
- Celebrate a team that will have absolute clarity about its purpose

Building Team Capacity

In the following sections I will cover specific steps that a senior supervisor can use to build their team's capacity. This should be a helpful step-by-step guide you can use after learning the theory sections above. Anything we attempt to do to improve our projects will depend on the time and capacity we have as a leader. Building team capacity is so important. Follow these steps to begin to create capacity, implement, and improve.

Step 1 - Know the Importance of Building the Team

Knowing the importance of building the team will increase your ability to create a "sticky" high-performance, high-retention culture that will encourage your people to engage with each other as they overcome multiple, large and complex problems. I want you to be able to go home with a good work/life balance with the knowledge that you're able to take care of your family and know the project is still moving forward. All of us in the construction industry can remember our early days as an intern or an engineer on a project and watching to see when the senior leadership went home. We waited to go home after they did for no good reason other than to match their departure time and look good to our boss. We regretted staying, arrived home late, burnt out, feeling like our time was not spent where it should have been. It was mentally taxing, but we continued in the cycle.

The effects of an unhealthy culture, like staying because the leader stayed late, must be reduced, minimized, or completely eliminated for those who are coming up in the industry. If we want a "sticky" high-performance, high-retention culture, then we have to support good balance and health. Team balance will not happen naturally; we must be intentional about it. To create balance you, as the leader, must focus on stability.

Have you ever driven a car that has an unbalanced tire? At lower speeds the effects of being unbalanced might not appear, but when speed increases to forty or fifty miles an hour, you can feel the car shake and shimmy. If you push the car above sixty miles an hour, it might even feel like the car will fly off the road because it's shaking so badly.

A team cannot progress and have continuous improvement on-site if they don't have the bandwidth. Can you imagine a team being really high functioning and clicking if they are not balanced and stable? It would be like driving on those unbalanced wheels. You might get somewhere but the drive would be bone jarring and exhausting. A team that is united in health and function can achieve results beyond their combined individual contributions. When teams are in "a state of flow," members have superior operational control of their areas on-site, their assignments are locked in and they are functioning as a team, so that they can win every day. A team, like a wheel, will not be able progress smoothly if they are not balanced.

Team balance is the first thing leaders get to focus on. Nothing else will work without it. Entrepreneur Richard

Branson says, "Customers aren't first. Your people are first and then they'll take care of your customers." I agree with that entirely. If you have healthy people, those people will have the ability to create remarkable experiences for your customers. The best way to do that is by taking care of your employees first. There are a couple of things that can really make this intentional. First...

Step 2 - Get to Know Each Other

In *The Five Dysfunctions of a Team* by Patrick Lencioni there is a pattern teams go through for the stages of team building. First, create trust, have healthy conflict, set goals together, and hold each other accountable to those goals. Once the team works through these steps, the team will perform. Patrick Lencioni does an absolutely fantastic job of talking about how this model works and how teams can perform if they start with trust. But it's very difficult to get to the trust part. Most of the time, teams can only begin to build trust if they get to know each other first. To build familiarity use a tool called, "This Is Me." The questionnaire, if answered sincerely and with detail, will help team members know and understand one another.

Let me explain just a little bit about how this works. The top question on the form begins "The one thing I need from my team is…" The next is "Like most people, I'm pretty easy to get along with, but these are my hot buttons… You can help me by…" These additional questions are intended to really make you think about who you are and how you work and illuminate yourself and your work habits to your teammates.

Here are all the questions for your reference:
- What are the types of communication that help you the most with your team? (Explain)
- You try to be easy to have a good relationship with, but like most people, you have a few "hot buttons." Very briefly, what are they? (Explain)

- What is your biggest strength?
- How can we encourage you in your strengths?
- What is your biggest weakness?
- How can we help you overcome your weakness?
- How do you like interaction when you have reached a point of stress?
- When a team member has identified a potential blind spot in your role, how would you like feedback?
- What is one thing you want us to know?
- What do you value? (Explain)
- What activities and assignments give you back more energy than you put into them? (Explain)
- What do you want to accomplish at work? (Explain)
- What would be success in your opinion? (Explain)
- What would be personally fulfilling in your role? (Explain)
- What do you expect from the people you work with? (Explain)
- What behaviors should they expect from you? (Explain)

Let me give you a quick example about this method. On one of my former teams, there was a person who just seemed to hate me. We filled out a questionnaire that was similar to "This is Me." On his form he stated, "I hate emails, I think they're irresponsible forms of delegation and I don't like them." This was a surprise to me because I loved emails. I would get a hit of dopamine every time I sent one—even though they wasted so much time. Once I found out about him not liking emails, I stopped sending them to him. Instead, I would go to his desk and say, "Hey, dude, you got a minute to talk? I just have this question" or, "Hey, could we partner about this?" And our relationship improved so much we ended up being pretty close by the end of the job. A complete turnaround happened once I knew him a little better.

There was nothing, absolutely nothing, that would break down the brick wall that was between us because he hated the fact that I sent emails because "when air is charged with emotions, an attempt to teach is often perceived as a form of judgment and rejection." - Steven Covey. When we were in the same room, area, meeting and I said a word, it was as if somebody sucked the air out of the room until I made the effort to resolve the email issue. I've witnessed many occasions when people dislike each other, don't get along, or don't trust each other. The trick is to better understand each other and be more patient but also act in a way that makes the other person feel safe. It takes an exchange of communication. We all need to feel listened to.

This is just a small example of what you can do to bring people together and build rapport to build understanding. If you choose a different method, please remember that people need to know how to safely communicate with each other in order to build trust. They need to know what things may stand in the way of building trust. And finally, they need to get past it. Another really great tool is the use of...

Step 3 - Personality Assessments

A personality profile helps illuminate your tendencies and traits. Contrary to some beliefs, personalities are not permanent and thus the profile can never be 100% accurate. It is, however, a remarkably effective tool to start a conversation that helps us dig deeper into who someone is and what they care about. We hear a lot in the industry, especially on IPD projects and in Lean circles, about using Enneagram, Working Genius, Myers-Briggs, the DISC profile, or StrengthsFinder tools. I personally believe in these tools and have taken all of them. I love using them and my personal favorite is the Meyers Briggs assessment. However, an assessment must be paired with a questionnaire asking someone who they are and what they want.

I know there are some out there who say these personality assessments are too broad to tell me who I am. Did they tell me who I am? No. Did they help me find out who I am? Absolutely. So before you get too wrapped up into which test is the best or most accurate, I would suggest you use the one that can help you assess yourself. For me, Meyers Briggs and Strengthsfinder did the trick. Actually, all of them combined painted a great picture for me.

These tests profile you and indicate your dos and don'ts, strengths and weaknesses, and suggestions on how to interact with other personality types. It is amazing how in-depth you can get and how accurate the information can be when used as a quick point of reference and conversation starter.

As a point of practice on my teams, I utilize player cards which combine a few of the tests like DISC, Myers-Briggs, StrengthsFinder, and the highlights from the "This Is Me" document. With permission, I post these player cards on the wall in the conference room or near team member's desks. I find them very helpful in creating connections and safe pathways to communication.

One time, after doing a Myers-Briggs assessment, somebody's results showed they preferred to stay in the moment and be a little bit reactive and avoidant of long-term planning, scheduling, or organization. One of the suggestions on the personality profile was for them to match themselves with someone on the team who does like long-term planning, organization, and setting goals so it would balance out the team. We did just that and the team thrived. I have seen this happen over and over in my career. When we balance the team's personalities, we get great results. Knowing each other (and acting on that information) creates balance; understanding each other really helps us to create...

Step 4 - Safe Communication and Healthy Conflict

People will talk to each other and have difficult conversations as long as the conversation feels more possible than putting up with the irritant. As a leader you need to develop safe pathways of communication; your people must develop an approach to speak to one another that creates safety and openness. The communication pathways between the team members must convey a feeling of safety so each team member can feel free to get to know one another. Destructive interactions will not grow the team dynamic.

Let me give you an example. There was a new job with eight people on the team that were not new to the company, but new to working with each other. When they got together, they would avoid conflict in a team meeting. However, outside of the team meetings they had a lot to say to each other and about each other. They didn't dive in or help one another. The side conversations really broke down their trust in one another. I couldn't control them or what they said. I couldn't tell them they shouldn't confide in others outside the team or have exclusive buddies to talk to within the team. What I could suggest and encourage was building trust with one another by telling each other in team meetings what they would normally say to their confidant. They began practicing this in meetings and reported later that there was very little they would not be willing to share with each other in the group. They had practiced healthy conflict and normalized it among the team.

The key is to start using the "This Is Me' document and the personality profiles to address things the team would normally not address. This will only happen by making it intentional and practicing in team meetings. That is why I recommend having feedback or mining for conflict on the agenda of every team meeting. If you do this, and if you practice, you can get to a point where you actually have healthy conflict within a team. Now, let's make sure...

Step 5 - Roles are Clearly Defined

In the early stages of team development it is very important to make sure that our people are in their proper roles; not roles as in titles, silos, politics, or bureaucracy. Instead I'm referring to an awareness of responsibility. Does everyone on the team know how they add value, where they're supposed to be, their responsibilities in the project, where they are supposed to be stationed, and what they're supposed to be doing to contribute to the team?

In addition to making the scope breakouts visual, make sure that everyone knows that we have both scope and geographical assignments and control. That means all scopes and areas are covered. It's very important that people are in their roles and the team knows the areas and scopes each person is covering. Though the roles are clearly defined, they're defined with thin lines. Thin lines mean a team would benefit from the balance that occurs from knowing what every other team member does. If the PM is gone, the project superintendent should be able to lead the OAC. If the project superintendent is gone, the project manager should be able to do the schedule update to cover some of those trade partner planning meetings. We are striving to create nimble teams, with members able to step in, lean in and take care of things as needed. We never want to hear, "Oh, so and so is gone. I have no idea how to do this. You're going to have to wait until they get back, Sorry." Rather the response should be, "Oh yeah, so and so is gone, but I can cover that for you; it's no big deal," without fear of stepping on each other's toes. Be nimble and step in when needed.

We must remember that even though we have people running point for certain things, problems belong to the entire team. Everyone owns the schedule, the finances, the field, and the office collectively. At any time we must be open to ask each other about the status of their responsibilities. Be prepared to help. Remember, we have people running point for scopes and areas, but we lead as an integrated team. Initially, this is the key step for building a team. All other successes are feasible when we have a foundation of people running point for the different scopes and areas yet lead as an integrated team. We set up amazing reporting cycles, healthy conflict, and goals, but those systems are all built upon the integrated team and everyone knowing their proper roles on a project. I would encourage you and your team to immediately have a little brainstorming session to identify roles both geographically and by scope. You must remember that you cannot properly or easily control a site unless you have the geographical areas covered and controlled. Map it out early and it will work if you work it as a team.

Step 6 - Healthy Partnerships

The project manager and superintendent are complementary roles which must support each other. On one of the last projects I ran directly as a superintendent, the project manager and I did not get along. I didn't trust him. His style was not like mine. We didn't do anything in a similar way. We didn't see things the same way. I didn't trust his motives. It was a rocky start. In hindsight, I think most of it was my fault. When I began to consider how we were going to improve the relationship, a couple of things came to mind. I started to wonder if I should complain to the project executive. Should I start causing trouble? Should I fight with him? Should I just bottle it all up? What should I do? Then I asked myself, "How am I going to make this situation better? Why don't I trust this guy? Why does he bother me?" Looking back on it I can see that I was being a control freak and I wanted most of the control over everything.

Eventually the solution came to me. "Okay, if I start complaining, it's going to make a mess. If I start fighting, it's not going to be productive. If I don't figure this out, it's going to be unhealthy". So I decided, "You know what, I'm going to give him the benefit of the doubt. I'm going to work to make his job easier. If something needs to be done, I'm going to get it done right away. If I need something, I'm going to be super respectful about it. I'm going to make sure that I never, ever bad-mouth him. I'm going to make sure that I just give, give, give, give, and give. I'm going to give up control." From that point our relationship started to improve and it was because I started to give and built trust.

Because I started to build a rapport with him, he was more apt to look at my good side, to trust me, and to give me more latitude. He began to praise me and never bad-mouth me. He supported the things that I had done and the things that I was trying to do. That's when I realized that he and I still didn't do things the same way. We still didn't think the same way; we were still different people. But the relationship was just fantastic. He would go into a meeting and say, "Hey, Jason's the expert about that. We need to really look at this. Let's ask him." He became my biggest advocate.

You must have a great relationship with the project manager. In fact, everyone on the project needs to have a great relationship with the other members of the team. We have discussed how to build these relationships, but there must be some intentionality behind building these relationships. You must decide that you want a good relationship with your counterpart and create a power pairing. So, if you are in a PE/FE duo, PE/assistant super duo, or a PM/super duo, you must get along and work in unison; you must create a power pairing. You are obligated to make that relationship right for the good of the project. You may have to schedule intentional meetings, go out to lunch every week, or explore other options, but it must be done. It must be done because the PM and super pairing is crucial in the leadership of the project. There must be unity, clarity, synchrony, and energy within your pairing. If you do not have these qualities within the pairing, you will always be pulling in different directions, and portions of your project will fail.

Step 7 - Widen Your Circle

Transparency is crucial to a team. I'll give you a quick story and tell you why transparency is a big deal. I once went to a project and felt uncomfortable because I wasn't used to being transparent. I wanted to continue to play all my cards close to my vest and show none of them. I wasn't used to things being out in the open, and I wasn't very happy when I was pushed in that direction. The PM on the project would share information quickly; if something happened that the project executive needed to know about he would send out a quick email or text with the news to everyone on the team. I remember thinking, "Dude, what are you doing? Why are you being that way? You can't keep making me look bad." His answer was, "No, we're a team and there are certain things that need to be shared with other parts of the team. The project executive or the project director needs to know these things, and there's no shame in sharing them." Although I understood the concept, I had a real problem with it because I felt diminished in my role. Only later did I get to understand the magic of it all.

The project manager was creating a culture of widening the circle. Widening the circle means we loop in other members of our team and do not judge anyone for either having or dealing with problems. The concept is that we deal with problems together. People are judged on how they respond to and interact within the team to correct the problems as a group.

I'll give you examples of some behaviors. Let me start with some of the low-hanging fruit.

The Safety Walk

In this culture, I experienced safety directors who would come and walk the job. They would have pictures and a report of things that needed to be fixed on-site. My first response was territorial. "Why is somebody walking my job?" But I soon realized what was taking place. The email with the pictures and the corrective items would go to the leaders of the company, other important people, the PM, and the entire team. I expected the worst at first, but nobody ever said a negative word about the issues on the report. I did get a forceful call once though where I was asked what I was doing about these things. When I opted not to respond immediately, I was told, "Hey Jason, it's not a big deal that these issues exist. We simply want to know that in twenty-four hours all the items will be corrected or what the plan is to correct the lingering items. We want actions and a plan to take care of our people on-site." This request came as a surprise to me, but the next time they walked I was ready. When the report came out, our field team fixed all the items and when I replied it said, "Hey, we took care of everything, There's one item that's lingering, but we have the materials coming and we'll fix it tomorrow morning." Guess what kind of response I got? "Great. Great job. Great, absolutely fantastic!" I learned that problems belong to the team and the main focus of the team must be to correct problems as a team in a timely manner. That's just one little example of that remarkable culture at work.

The Fire Truck

A fire truck came down the road through the site and had a hard time getting through one of our fire access roads on the west end which caused them to have to detour around the other side of the block. Unfortunately, I decided it was not a big deal. I did not go see what was wrong. I did not tell the team, and I did not tell the owner. I didn't widen my circle. Then I got a call from the project executive. He said, "Hey, Jason. The owner just called me and told me about this fire truck incident. What's the deal? Why didn't I know about it?" I started going down the rabbit hole of "Well, this is what happened and blah, blah, blah." He said, "Jason, I love you, bro. I don't care that it happened. Every project has problems. Why didn't you tell me?" I didn't have a good answer. I told him, "I didn't think you needed to know, and it wasn't a big deal to me." And then he told me this: "I am a part of your team. Just because I'm a project executive doesn't give you the right to leave me out of pertinent information. I was surprised by the owner and didn't know what to say because you didn't circle in your team. I am your team member and you aren't trusting me to be a part of your team." And that's when it all changed for me. I realized that while there are certain small and low-risk things you can take care of yourself, most of the issues should be taken care of with the team because everyone owns the problems on the project. Then there are some things from a cost, owner, or risk perspective when we really need to circle in project executives, project stakeholders, the safety director, the general superintendent, and possibly the owner. They're part of our team and we should trust them.

The Fire Alarm

There was a day when the fire alarm went off in the adjacent building, and we didn't know if it was our fault or not. I immediately sent a text to the owner, the owner's rep, project executive, and the rest of the team. As we swarmed at the adjacent building to offer support, we found out it was an unscheduled test. The facilities manager for the building sent a compliment to the director of construction and we received feedback that we were acting like a high performing team. That is when we started to build trust with the owner. No matter what issue came up, anyone on the team who needed to know would be notified. We created a culture where people would immediately notice a problem and widen their circle and bring other people in as a resource. It worked remarkably.

If I had a crane coming, I would tell the safety director, "Hey, FYI next week we've got a crane coming, a really big one. We're setting it up. I just want to let you know." If there was a big issue I was dealing with, I would text the project executive and the field ops director and say, "Hey, this is what we're doing; if you have anything to add, please advise." Everything on-site was analyzed to see if we needed to widen the circle and get other people into the group or not; we also learned to default to widening. Even if certain people likely didn't need to know, we would tell the team in order to ensure everyone was up-to-date. That is an empowering, beautiful, unburdening philosophy. When a team can really learn to widen their circle, it communicates that somebody is a part of the team and deserves to take part in team decisions.

Step 8 - Team Coverage

Sometimes we need to widen our circle when we are on-site, and sometimes we need to widen our circle and let someone cover for us. Let me ask you some questions, and please take the opportunity to respond. How much of the plan does the superintendent understand? Let's just say it's one hundred percent. Now, how much of the project plan do the foremen understand? Would you say forty percent? Sixty? How much does the worker understand the project plan from a percentage standpoint? Is it five percent? Ten? I ask because we have to increase these percentages. If you think about the project engineer or the project manager knowing anything less than eighty or ninety percent, you'll realize that spells trouble. These percentages all have to increase for us to be able to have the right coverage, supervision, and effectiveness on-site.

What if all the percentages of knowledge rose at each level? Could the team then act in unison? Could the team cover for each other when needed? Could they spot for somebody else? Could they supervise work on a Saturday? And the answer is yes. We have to increase the percentage of what people know and understand about the plan so the team can lean in and support each other to fill in the gaps in the event someone is absent. Everyone knows that in construction, you work a lot of hours. In fact, when I was young, I researched construction management and saw this message "If you want to engage in an intense, fast-paced career that will take a lot of hours, then construction management is for you." It takes a lot of time. People have asked what the ideal amount of time is. I think fifty to sixty hours a week is the sweet spot. Sixty is a little heavy, but fifty-five hours may be just right. The point here is that we must cover for each other so we can work the right amount of hours, at the right times, and in the right way.

I've heard people say, "You know, my wife, she tells me she doesn't need me home, that it's fine if I have to work. She's got it covered." But under this false, well-intentioned harmony, I bet a more truthful answer might be "You know, I really need you at home on Wednesdays for activities. I really need you on Thursdays to take the kids to soccer practice or Saturdays are sacred for our family." There are duties, responsibilities, and pleasures given to us by our home life that deeply enrich our minds, bodies, and relationships. This is important not only for you, but also to your employer who is paying for a whole individual to show up and do their best.

You must be emotionally, spiritually, and physically healthy when you come to work. You are paid to be someone who is able to come to work and put everything into what you have with the right balance and mental fortitude. The harmony of a home and family life has better odds if you have the quantitative time to give it. That doesn't mean that we have to give our whole lives over to our family, partners, and pets, it just means there are key points that can help us nourish our home life.

Finding the individual balance that works for a person's family is ideal, and I like to put it into an Excel sheet where Monday, Tuesday, Wednesday, Thursday, and Friday are listed across the top. Daily hours are listed on the left. I then ask each person to indicate optimal arrival and departure times for work. A team member might say, "My wife doesn't care if I work late on Monday or Tuesday since the kids have other things to do, but on Wednesday, I need to be home at five-thirty. Thursday is pretty flexible, but my family really needs me home on Friday by three-thirty." The rest of the team enters their schedule the same way. Once everyone has populated their Excel spreadsheet with family time, personal time, and other leader standard work, team members will be able to identify which days certain individuals will open the site and cover orientations, and what days an individual can close the site and cover that night in case of an emergency. This will prevent supers from having to always work long hours and feel unsupported by the team, and it will enable each person to work a reasonable amount of hours. Modifications are only made when coordinated because of a schedule change or a person being on PTO. The completed, agreed upon schedule is called a coverage schedule.

A coverage schedule will not happen unless you are intentional about it. Once you have a coverage schedule, post a visual schedule on the wall in the conference room and have the team hold each other accountable to the schedule. Things get remarkable when the team begins to call each other out if they are not caring for their family or personal time. It is not uncommon in cultures like this to hear something like, "Hey John, isn't it your night to go home? What can I cover for you so you can leave?" That is when things really get fun and balanced.

Step 9 - Knowing What to Cover

There have been many projects in the past that have had team coverage schedules yet nobody follows the team coverage schedule. They ignore it and go their separate ways. Things descend into chaos and the team starts to burn itself out again. Burnout usually happens because people do not know what to cover even if they follow the schedule, and the super doesn't trust anyone to stay and supervise. This can also happen within other roles and scopes. So the next key question arises: Do the people covering understand what they're doing? Do the team members trust each other in general to cover each other's scopes? Does the team understand why the team coverage schedule is impactful?

Once the team develops a team coverage schedule, each individual (especially within the power pairings) must communicate the plan to every foreman, superintendent, engineer, laborer, and worker on-site, within their scope and scope coverage. The site personnel must know, understand, and follow the plan for each day. What would it look like if a worker could arrive at work with full knowledge of what's going on and set up their day with the materials, instructions, space, cleanliness, and organization on-site? The site personnel would know what to do, the burden on the leadership team would be reduced, and team coverage would thrive! How can a worker find a utopia that includes consistency, predictability, safety, support, money, and awesome productivity? Part of the answer is to plan with the foreman and communicate with all the personnel on the jobsite.

This utopia starts on the office team's scrum boards. The plan for the next day must be visual for office operations. Take the time to get everyone onboard so they can see as a group, know as a group, and act as a group. Then the site leadership team needs to plan together with the foreman and communicate daily with the personnel on the jobsite. An afternoon foreman huddle enables the team to make plans on a single document for the next day that clearly outlines the tasks to complete, what deliveries are coming and where they go, what inspections are taking place, and all other material aspects of the project plan for the following day. During the next morning huddle, the daily plan is communicated with the site personnel. This allows the site leadership group to cover for each other since the plan is always repeated and communicated and everyone is up-to-date and aware of what needs to be done. Taking time to plan for the next day ensures that personnel are prepared and you can get your people home to have a work/life balance.

Without a plan and clear, concise communication to the workers, chaos ensues. When the site is in chaos, people are left to walk around searching for materials or not knowing what to do. You are re-coordinating over and over again with various groups, stopping workers and crews, and halting production to change direction and aligning personnel back to a plan that was hidden from them. This means you end up working late, fighting fires, and ruining the schedule for the team. Every team must know what to cover, how to cover it, how to communicate it, and then be able to perform well in the absence of another team member. For more information about Scrum in the office and the creation of day plans, reference Construction Scrum by Felipe Engineer and The Lead Builder by Keyan Zandy and Joe Donarumo.

Step 10 - Team Health Survey

The team health survey can be an amazing tool to create capacity among a team. There are many examples and templates of team health surveys in the industry. Which one you use is not as important as the fact that you use one. The goal is to create capability. A good survey can be really helpful in gauging whether or not the team is performing optimally, because again, we need to bring problems to the surface to maintain team balance and health.

In this book I have included a team health survey you can use to gauge the health and capacity of your team. The main topics included in the template are foresight and planning, clarity and alignment, and balance and stability. These topics create a foundation for operational excellence and running the business. This evaluation tool is best used when everybody grades each item on a scale of 1 to 100. After the team finishes the grading exercise, the scores are aggregated so the team can see the overall scores and identify areas of improvement that will create additional capacity. The best practice is to score this on a weekly or monthly basis and see how the team is trending. If there are items under seventy-five percent, the team should put energy into solving to create more balance and stability among the team.

Team Assessment Items

You cannot manage what you cannot measure, and you cannot measure what you cannot see. Teams are intentionally built so performance can be seen and measured. When performance is measured, performance improves. When performance is measured and reported, the rate of improvement accelerates. Here are some items that can be measured on your team:

Category 1 - Balance and Stability

- Are team members in their proper roles?
- Is the work and level of responsibility leveled among roles properly?
- Do all leaders have and follow Leader Standard Work?
- Are standard schedules set for the team weekly to support home life?
- Does the team understand each team member's personality?
- Does each team member have a work/life balance?
- Are team members meeting their career goals?
- Are all team members feeling healthy at work?
- Are team members overburdened with work and responsibility?
- Does the team engage in healthy conflict?
- Is there good chemistry among the team?

- Does the team have high morale?
- Does the team have a good meeting system?
- Are critical issues dealt with among the team effectively?
- Is there a healthy relationship with the owner?
- Is there a healthy relationship with the designer?
- Does the team focus on and get training weekly?
- Are design changes overburdening the onsite team?

Category 2 - Foresight and Planning

- Is there an effective master schedule for the project?
- Was the plan and schedule complete before NTP?
- Does the team make contingency plans ahead of time?
- Is there a good system to track procurement and purchasing?
- Are ⅓ and ⅔ milestones on track?
- Is the team learning by visiting similar projects?
- Is there good visual planning on-site?

Category 3 - Clarity and Alignment

- Are milestones established and clear to the team?
- Is there a strenuous performance goal or milestone for the team to rally to?
- Does the team know what the customers want and need?
- Is this clarity scaled to the entire project team effectively?
- Are all levels of leadership in the field office aligned in direction and purpose?

- Are safety and quality expectations clear to everyone?
- Is there an identified path to the end?
- Does the team know what one thing the project must focus on now?
- Is the plan and schedule visually communicated to the project?
- Does everyone on site understand project operations?

Category 4 - Business Operations

- Does the project have good cash flow?
- Is there good risk identification and mitigation?
- Is there a good profit strategy on the project?
- Is the change management system working on-site?
- Is there enough estimating help for changes?
- Are contingencies well managed?
- Is the team creating a raving fan out of the client?

Category 5 - Operational Excellence

- Is Lean used as a development system on the project?
- Is the project clean?
- Does the project team have control of the project?
- Is the project safe?
- Are the craft workers producing a quality product?
- Are crews hitting production?
- Is the team tolerating bad behavior?
- Is the current and updated information being communicated real-time to the field?

If your team can intelligently and authentically self-evaluate according to those categories, you will be able to identify immediate areas for improvement and increase your team effectiveness.

Remarkable Communication

I once asked a Lean expert what he saw as the most common problem among businesses. Without any hesitation he said, "Communication. There is always a communication problem." This put things into perspective for me. Everything we have discussed up to this point—leadership, teaming, meetings, and building team capacity—can only be activated with good communication skills. I've included some tips to help you, as the project leader, communicate in a remarkable way. First, we need to...

Tip 1 - Understand the Importance of Communication

Do you want to increase communication on your project? Do you want to have healthier conversations? Would you like some safe pathways for communication among your team members? Would you like to grasp just a little bit better this concept of communication? If so, then these are for you.

Patrick Lencioni said, "There is no such thing as too much communication." I hope you believe that. Again, nothing is activated among team members without communication. I don't think schedules are healthy or valuable if they're not communicated all the way to the workers. I don't think budgets are effective without communication. I don't think any project tool or system is valuable unless they get communicated across the board.

I once talked my wife into going to a Rapport Leadership International 2.5 day course called Power Communication. It was an immersion course on how to be a better leader and communicate effectively. I can't do it justice with my explanation, but trust me, it was a fantastic experience. While I was there, I participated in an exercise that really hooked me and caused a paradigm shift. I became aware of how differently people communicate with one another. Here is a rule of thumb: You have to assume that even though you are technically speaking the same language, the differences between what you say, show, and understand can be just as different as if you and the other person were from different planets. If you don't believe me, just dig deep into any long-standing relationship. You may find that a couple married twenty years can still misunderstand most of what is said or shown.

One of the exercises took place in a closed room using Legos that required three participants. A Lego set was assembled in a particular way, and one member of the three-person team (the observer) was able to go into the room and look at the Legos without taking notes. The observer could see what it looked like, but could not touch it. The observer was then instructed to leave the room and explain to another member of the team (the communicator) what the Lego set looked like. Following that, the communicator was told to go into a different room and explain to the third member of the team (the builder) how to assemble the Legos in the same manner as they appeared in the original room as described by the observer. The mission was to build an identical structure of legos. The observer never talked to the builder, the communicator never saw the original building, and the builder had to rely only on team communication to build it right. It was a super fun experience.

And so we began. My role was that of a communicator. I had a great team member assigned as the observer. Mike and I had gotten along just fine before this. I waited while he went in to inspect the Lego set. When he came back and started explaining the way the structure was built, I noticed his eyes went up and to the left, staring into the air while using what to me sounded like rambling, disconnected words. I was trying to get him to be specific. "Show me what should I do? Where does the red block go? Where does the blue block go? Use your hands to show me." Still looking up at an imaginary figure, he tried to tell me, "Well, the red is on the other side of the...well, this block is on that side of that." So I said, "No, no, no, show me on my hands," and I put my hands out in front of me. "Mike, pretend my right hand is the blue block and my left hand is a red block. Where do they go?" A look of panic showed on his face and then he looked up again and started rambling. I almost grabbed his face to make him focus on my hands. I asked again, "Where is the blue block and where is the red one?" He couldn't do it so I gave up and just attempted to make sense of his words. I didn't understand what he was saying and he did not understand my need to visualize the structure. We were a mess. I remember being so frustrated and thinking "Oh, my goodness. This is a nightmare." We didn't even get halfway close on putting the thing together. Neither of us could give the other what they needed to build successfully. And this same scenario plays out every single day of our lives aside from the superficially light conversations when people really aren't paying attention anyway. All real communication is difficult.

This taught me that there are different types of communication that people value and use differently. People learn visually, audibly, and kinesthetically. And knowing that humans are complex systems, there are likely a million or more ways that people string these styles together to observe and communicate. As a lead superintendent, these concepts will help you when scaling excellence and scaling communication in your position. We have the task of communicating a plan to visual, kinesthetic, and auditory learners— communicators—who may be begging us to understand their style of communication. We have to use visual maps, we have to talk about it, we have to get out there in huddles and communicate with our bodies and show people. We need to use all the communication tools in our toolbelt. If we do, we will be able to do our main job as a senior supervisor—communicate the plan!

Tip 2 - Create a Culture of Communication

Communication is a culture, and cultures are built with little micro-actions and little moments. It isn't so much the large things, but the small things that build trust and create the culture of the organization. And we all know that culture will eat strategy every day. So we need to get the culture right, and to get the culture right, we must focus on the small actions and habits of the team. Why is this important? Because we need to see as a group, know as a group, and act as a group on a construction site to really win. Please remember that there is no insignificant interaction. Every interaction matters because it shapes the culture. As a project leader you must correct toxic communication and praise productive communication.

Tip 3 - Be Aware of Different Communication Styles

We know there are different types of learners and different types of communicators. A more auditory style focuses on listening. This is when we prefer words and explanations. When we use a more kinesthetic style, we prefer to touch things with our hands. We are more physical. We want to go, do, and experiment. When we favor the visual style, we may want to stand back and look, visualizing things with our eyes, and picturing it in our minds.

It is important to understand these differing styles so we can connect with other team members. There may be another team member or foreman in your meetings who you think is obstinate and argumentative. What if he or she just doesn't communicate the way you do and that person is frustrated? Can you adjust your approach, connect, and really partner with him or her?

Tip 4 - Value Introverts and Extroverts

In addition to different learning styles, we also encounter introversion and extroversion. There are marked differences between introverts and extroverts. There are some fantastic books like *The Introvert Advantage: How Quiet People Can Thrive in an Extrovert World* by Marti Olsen Laney and *Quiet: The Power of Introverts in a World That Can't Stop Talking* by Susan Cain that have shed some light on the value of introverted thinking. I am convinced that we need to use the skills of introverts in our industry, and to do so we need to communicate well with introverts. Extroverts may need to do a little bit of adapting and introverts may need to speak up more.

The following is a list of notes I took from reading *The Introverted Advantage*, that as an extrovert, I found helpful.

1. First, Introverts do not think like extroverts. Extroverts think outside of their head, introverts think inside. So don't be shocked when you have to actually ask what an introvert is thinking.

2. Introverts are not as susceptible to praise on the whole. You may need to stick to facts when praising good work, and don't get frustrated if you don't get an emotional or visible reaction.

3. Introverts take longer to think, not because they are slow, but because they think about the entire process step-by-step. Introverts need a sanctuary and quiet time. They sometimes need to say, "I'll get back to you." Don't be afraid to give an introvert twenty-four or more hours to get back to you. If you do, you will likely get a top-notch answer.

4. Introverts don't like interruption. This is important because Introverts are outnumbered three to one and can feel pushed, overwhelmed, and overstimulated. Make sure they have their productive and focus time.

5. Introverts can go unseen and unrecognized which can be mentally unhealthy. Introverts need to be drawn out because they need more connection in their relationships, even at work. We need to keep connecting in the right moments to provide that connection.

6. Introverts can remain at a task longer than extroverts. They have more focus and endurance. This characteristic is very helpful to the team and should be supported.

7. Introverts are great advisors and doers because they are thoughtful and steady. You will want someone with this characteristic on your team so you can make better decisions and implement well.

8. Introverts are detailed and focused and deal best with one or two projects. Keep this in mind when dividing responsibilities among the team.

I hope these insights are helpful. The biggest difference between introversion and extroversion is energy. The question is how do we recharge? If you put an extrovert in a group of people or in a social environment, they might be physically tired, but they gain energy by being around others. If you put an introvert in that same situation, it might drain their energy and result in a need for quiet time and rest. Does that mean that extroverts always speak up more? No. Does that mean that introverts don't speak up enough? No. There are no generalizations or stereotypes here, but rather a recognition of distinct personality traits that need to be taken into consideration when we work together so we can connect and support one another. Can you adapt your style to the other end of the spectrum?

Tip 5 - Communicate for Understanding

Nobody gets any points for merely communicating something. We have to communicate for understanding. Let me give you some examples. What if you go out to the field and fill out a crane plan with the crews, but they don't follow it. Should you ask, "Why are they so obstinate or disobedient?" or should you question whether your communication was for understanding. Unless the crew understood it and was committed to following through, the attempt at communicating the crane plan was a wasted effort. You have not earned the right to ask for teamwork or compliance unless the expectations were clear. The paperwork was not to CYA or create a historical record. Paperwork or plans only have significance if they do their intended job—to communicate expectations.

A second example is orientations. What if you put thirty people through orientation and check the box? Questions remain. Did they understand what was communicated? Did they pass a test? Were they able to provide the right answers? Do they know how to put together a pre-task plan? The success isn't in the telling; it's in the comprehension. We get off-track when we satisfy ourselves with "Well, I told them," The only thing "I told them" means is that we didn't care enough to actually follow through to make sure everyone understood, cared, and had what they needed to execute.

As senior superintendents and leaders out on our construction projects, It is your job to make sure that everyone understands what you tell them. That means you stay there, stick with it, ask questions, test them, and prove it out until you know for a fact that these wonderful people understand the expectations, understand the culture, and have what they need.

Tip 6 - Build Open Offices

I warn everybody every stinking time about not building separate offices, and people keep ignoring me (except for the wise ones). The wisdom of using open offices has been proven over and over and over again. I once read a LinkedIn post that I can't help but rant about here. The man was talking about putting the nail in the coffin about open, integrated big room spaces not working. He cited a study showing that open and collaborative big room spaces increase the number of text messages, meetings, and conversations. His point was that these environments create more waste, more messaging time, and more meetings. He said, "Open offices do not work because they create waste, and hopefully this concept of big rooms will soon go away." And I thought to myself, "Wow, how untrue is that?" The open big room environment is to create a throughput of communication as a team to solve problems for the field, not to individually silo and be individually productive. We want the workers to be productive. Offices are not designed so somebody can go sit in a remote office and be efficient and productive and comfortable by themselves. The point of a team is to get things done collectively as a group and to increase the throughput of communication to solve problems. Project teams should discomfort themselves so they can comfort the workers. They comfort workers by getting them the tools, information, training, and time needed to do their work. To do that, the management team must collaborate. To collaborate, they must have the right non-siloed environment.

If you are in an integrated project delivery environment, in a big room environment, text messaging, phone calls, and verbal communication increases and does not create waste. Rather, it creates value for the workers in the field.

Anytime I see the director, executive, PM, or the senior super in their ivory castle with the door shut, I want to scream. Their seclusion is akin to putting a freshly baked cookie in a vault for safekeeping. Directors, executives, PMs, and senior supers are communicators and they must be out of their castle to perform. Most projects start out with these ivory castles. I always tell them, "Y'all, I wouldn't do that." In spite of the warning, they build their siloed walls anyway. And then sure enough, halfway through the project, somebody somewhere, even if they're not brave enough to say it themselves, will comment that those walls and doors break down trust and hurt the team. This concept is proven to make more communication and to reduce the siloed effect of individual efficiency. Now, if somebody wants to do production work for a day or two, by all means go off into one of the production pods or the conference room. But in order to communicate openly, these roles need to be carried out in an open space.

Tip 7 - Share Your Leader Standard Work and Goals

Leader Standard Work is a task that a leader must do daily and weekly because only they can and should do it. Neglecting to schedule this standard work will position someone in the thick of thin things causing he or she to ignore their duties and their future. How else would somebody know your standard work or respect it if you don't communicate it or share it? One of the best things I've ever done is to create my standard work and weekly work plan for the next week and share it. It communicates what jobs I'm going to, when I am helping with a proposal, and when I am working on focused tasks. Team members can see my schedule and know when to bug me or not to bug me. I used to get calls for eighteen different things during the day until I started sharing with everybody in my organization my work for the next week and my standard work. They began thinking, *I can fit it in here* or *I can talk to him then* or *I can do this myself since he is busy* or *hey, he's got some capacity here*. The amount of waste was measurably reduced, everyone was able to help protect my Leader Standard Work, and I was able to support them with key things when it was needed.

If you don't make the effort to communicate the individual standard work and personal goals, how will other people know? Personality assessments, profile cards, goals, and even things like family pictures could be printed and posted up on the wall to communicate your goals, what your standard work is, how you prefer interaction, and what is important to you. What drives the success of any project? People. So, if people are the most important aspect of any project, should the crucial aspects about people be the first thing we communicate? It should.

I hope these tips have helped. We will add to these for future revisions of this book. What would you add to the list?

Rules of Thumb When Building a Team:

If I expanded on every topic available for building teams, this would be a 10,000 book series. We don't need to do this; however, because most of us can quickly understand why certain concepts are important to a team. The list below is a summary of some of my favorite anchors when working with teams. I hope you enjoy them.

- Set and seize upon a few immediate performance-oriented tasks and goals to rally the team.
- Team members must be in their proper role. Get the right people on the team, and get team members in the right key seats.
- All key seats must have Leader Standard Work. LSW is the work that each leader must perform daily and weekly in their role to bring success to the project.
- Teams do well when they can do outside activities together.
- Activities are best remembered with pictures on the office walls.
- Make your office trailer feel like home. It should be so fun, inviting, and comfortable that people have a hard time leaving.
- Give first. Always help others in their role and support their career goals.
- Problems belong to the team. There is no such thing as one person's problem. There are only team problems.
- Widen the circle. When something happens and you need help, expand the circle of people you ask to help you.
- Major decisions are made as a team. There will be a leader who decides, but everyone gets to weigh in and buy in.
- No, "end-rounding." If you have something to say that is not sensitive and confidential, tell the person directly.

- Bring problems to the surface. Every team has problems. The best team brings them to the surface and deals with them.
- Open spaces encourage collaboration, transparency, and connection.
- Everyone is your equal on-site. Talk to them like you believe it.
- We all get what we tolerate. Teams should set very clear expectations about what will and will not be tolerated.
- Establish urgency and direction with weekly, monthly, or overall milestone goals.
- Select members based on skill and skill potential, not personalities.
- Pay particular attention to first meetings and actions of a team. Needs here will be needs in the future.
- Organize meeting systems so the team can communicate, collaborate, and connect in the right ways at the right times.
- Set some clear rules of behavior and post them on the wall when forming any social group.
- Exploit the power of positive feedback, recognition, and rewards. People work better with positivity.

Jobsite Support Ideas

If you really want to help, you need to dig deep to find out how the team is functioning. I remember a general superintendent once telling me, "Jason, you can tell a lot about how a team functions just by visiting the office, sitting down, and doing some work there. If you can do things like this and really find out how a team is working, you can help and support them." I've included a list to help you.

- **Attend a team meeting** - Attending a team meeting can be such a value adding experience. If you pay attention, you will be able to see if there is a goal, a leader, and the five key behaviors they need to be successful. The main thing is to see if they are holding each other accountable. If you do not see accountability, there may be a problem.

- **Take the leaders to lunch** - If you offer to take the leaders to lunch, you will either be turned down—which is a sign there is no cohesion or personal capacity—or they will go with you and you can observe any rapport or chemistry in their relationship.

- **Walk the job** - Walking the job will give you a good feel for the morale and health of the project. Consider stopping to talk to workers and foremen. If there is excellence on the project, they will tell you. If there is dysfunction, they will share.

- **Perform a team assessment survey** - Team health assessments can be very effective in finding problems on the project that should become a focus.

- **Encourage feedback** - While you are with the team, consider asking them to intentionally share feedback with each other. Sometimes folks just need a little extra push to step out of their comfort zone and provide feedback.

- **Dig deep into three things** - It is highly ineffective to visit a project and just look at things on a superficial level. When on-site, really dig into at least three things. When you lean in and attempt to assess or help the team with those things, you will see what the team is dealing with and the level of care they may need. This can be a big help in assessing where the team really is.

An Interview with Ricky Davenport

To illuminate my jobsite support ideas, I've included a transcript of an Elevate Construction podcast I did with Ricky Davenport. Ricky implemented the techniques you just read about and achieved amazing results. Let's find out what he had to say about implementing on this project:

Jason - Welcome to the Elevate Construction Podcast where we share stories of success from other professionals in our industry. My name is Jason Schroeder, and today we have Ricky Davenport, who will be talking to us about how to create a positive culture on our projects and share a number of other wonderful things with us today. Ricky Davenport is one of my favorite human beings. He is a project superintendent over a very large and very detailed project up in Pocatello, Idaho. And this building has some of the best high-end finishes I've ever seen. He has been able to create a wonderful culture on-site. I walked that job about two weeks ago, and literally found it to be the best in its class. So let me ask you your first question after you give us a little bit of information about your background.

Ricky - I grew up in Kirkland, Washington, and got into construction my junior year of high school. I fell in love with it, and I knew that's what I'd be doing my whole life. I worked in commercial construction. I met a girl from Blackfoot, Idaho, and got married and kept working construction as a carpenter, and got a chance to work for Okland at a BYU-Idaho project.

That was a great start for my career, I was working as carpenter and the finisher for Okland, and the economy tanked so I decided to go back to school while I was working for Okland and graduated in one of the worst economies in a recession, and got a call from Okland asking if I wanted to work for them. I took it, and it's been a blessing ever since.

Jason - Ricky, let me ask you a question. How long were you a carpenter? And a finisher, if you don't mind me asking?

Ricky - For Okland, It was two years, but before I worked for Okland, I framed commercially. I also ran a company for two and a half years.

Jason - And what degree did you go for?

Ricky - I got a Bachelor's in Construction Management.

Jason - Well, fantastic. I love it. How many kids do you have?

Ricky - I have six kids. They're the best. And a wonderful wife. And it can be done. You can be a great superintendent while managing all those roles.

Jason - Tell me about that because that's one of the biggest things we try to do. So expand on that if you don't mind. Give us a little history there.

Ricky - There's an ideal in construction you have to work eighty hour weeks or seventy hour weeks, and you have to yell at everyone and run the jobsite pointing fingers and really pushing work. But if you have a good plan and it's well communicated, you can make anything successful. You communicate that plan and get buy-in from everyone on-site. Not just from the superintendents, but all the way down to the general laborers on-site. They can feel the energy and positive reinforcement as well as the visual communication.

Jason - I think what we're going to find out throughout this podcast is that you've been able to share this plan and create stability on-site and get home for your wife. So let me ask you this, let me put you on the spot. Would your wife and kids say that you're home more?

Ricky - Oh yeah. And my team holds me accountable for that. That wasn't always the case earlier in my career; it's been a shift. But I've found that I'm more productive. I'm more ready and alert to the needs of the project as I manage my personal life.

Jason - I love that. And you also said you spent time in the scheduling department doing nothing but schedules for a time. Is that correct?

Ricky - Yeah. About seven months.

Jason - Seven months. Ricky is one of the best scheduling superintendents that I've been around. And I'd like to do a quick plug—If there's ever a way as a superintendent that you can get that scheduling experience and not have to broker that out to somebody else, it will greatly benefit your career. Every great superintendent and builder I know, knows how to schedule. Anything you want to add to that, Ricky?

Ricky - I think that's the key to anything because that's how you win in construction—through the schedule. That's how you stay on cost, that's how you create quality, and also have sufficient time to do what work is needed. But the schedule's been a big difference in my career, making a realistic schedule with buy-in and track into that schedule.

You can't use it as a bat, walking around with a bat beating the schedule across everyone's head, but instead really leading out and using it as a tool to create shared success among all the trade partners. Because they all have goals too. They all have dreams. And they have lives too. So we're on schedule, they're looking good, their boss is happy, their home life's good, and they do so much better at work. They're engaged, and they can lead the personnel in their company as well.

Jason - I love that. Let's get right into it. I'd like you to describe your role on the project, and then give us a brief description of what the project is. And then I'm going to point out some of the steps that you've taken to get it to the point it is today. So let's start by asking what your role is and having you describe the project.

Ricky - I'm a senior superintendent for a large project, like you said. I have two superintendents who work with me, an assistant superintendent, and a finish superintendent. And I also have an exterior envelope foreman as well as a concrete foreman and an interior carpenter foreman. So that's pretty much my team that I constantly work with and lead and guide.

It's been a great team on this project. We're running fast. And it's a beautiful thing to hit schedule, to hit quality, and have such a pleased client and design team. Some of the things that we've done on our project, like you said, is implement some Lean principles, which have changed the project completely, and changed my career completely.

This project is a religious building, and the finishes are really high. It's a beautiful building where the community has been very supportive and very excited for this building to be erected. They can be in a great community in their area and have a very involved client with an integrated design team. One of the best delivery methods we have on this project is that integrated design team.

We brought trade partners on really early to the project before design even started so we can work together and make a flawless building. Construction can proceed quickly and without change orders and a battle between contractor and design team. It's a team effort.

Jason - As you already said, have integrated design partners, an integrated extended team, integrated communication, integrated systems integrated goals. Integrated contracts, as much as you possibly can.

Integrated technology, integrated systems. So, that's one of them and how you treat people is another, but give me at least your top two best things that you've implemented on that project to create the kind of organizational health that you have?

And let me just first say that when you walk Ricky's job, first of all, it's clean and organized, which is the first key indicator. The other thing is it's good quality work. And then what I noticed about Ricky, and it's going to be uncomfortable for you because I'm bragging about you, but you walk through the halls and people turn around and look at him and he's like, "Hey, thanks for wearing your mask during COVID-19. Hey, great job on such and such. Hey, how are you doing? How's your family?"

There's a real connection there and people are just happy to be there. It's kind of like being at Disneyland. What are the two top things that you have done to create that culture?

Ricky - If we go to battle—and that's what we do in construction, we have rules of the game, but if we go to battle—we need to know who's on-site, we need to know the people, we know their dreams and their ambitions in life. And if you think you're too busy for that, then you're not leading your team. That's a big one. So just getting to know the feel, the people.

One of the key things that we've done on our project is our foreman huddles—that's at three o'clock every day. I think that's created more momentum and more teamwork than any other meeting I've ever been in. In most projects in construction, you have a superintendent meeting maybe once a week for a couple of hours and then you don't talk for a week and then get back together and realize a lot of the commitments weren't made, a lot of roadblocks were not communicated, and it just derails a project.

Every afternoon at three o'clock, all the foremen come in and we all talk. And it's mostly just, "Tell us your roadblocks. What's preventing you from hitting these milestones? Just tell us. We'll take care of it. We will stay up all night, all day. We will clear the road for you so you can have a successful project."

And at first they didn't get a buy-in. They're like "What? These guys are crazy. Do they really care?" Yeah, we care. Just communicate it. And as we opened up that line of communication, just things started happening. It was beautiful. I'm getting chills thinking about it. People were voicing their opinion. They didn't trust us at first, and our board was full of roadblocks every day. And we don't take the accountability from the trade partner, but we also work together to overcome those things to work through them.

It's great to go to the meeting and not say anything. It's a team meeting, but everyone's holding each other accountable. They're communicating in that meeting. They're clearing roadblocks. Not just design issues, but cleanliness, safety, and deliveries. It's their meeting. And as you meet, you can feel the energy, and if you make a safe place, we can really make fun of each other and laugh a lot, and realize it's not like construction. It can be fun if you make it.

And it's been a great thing. Because as you hit schedule and as you pull plan and as you work, you overcome all the obstacles that are in construction. Because if construction was easy, computers would do it, right? Monkeys could do it, right? Where is the need for the construction managers, the superintendents of the world, the project engineers, the field engineers, and project managers? They would not be needed.

But gratefully, construction's hard and it's difficult, and there's going to be roadblocks. There's going to be challenges. And as a team, as you overcome the challenges, it creates unity. With that unity and momentum, you can do anything, you can hit any schedule, you can overcome any roadblock as you work as a team.

Jason - What kind of pushback did you get in creating that culture? There are people all the time who will say, "I want to go do the worker huddles in the morning and talk to my guys, but what about COVID-19?" Or "I want to do the foreman huddle, but the trade partners say they don't want to do it." Or "I want to do weekly work planning on huddle boards, but there's some resistance there."

Ricky - Okay, I'll talk about one of my best friends. We didn't start out like that. The first day on the jobsite I showed him the cleanliness on-site, that the pipe should be on racks with wheels, and he didn't buy in. He kept laying his pipe everywhere and we kept taking it out of the building because he knows nothing touches the ground.

And he's getting mad. He's like, "Why do you have to be so difficult? I've never had this. Why are you being so crazy?" And I was like, "I'm not crazy, I love you, man. I just can't have it. We've got to be clean." And that's how it started, and it was maybe a little rougher than I'm communicating, but it was frustrating.

And you should see now. Everything is organized. Everything is perfect. His work goes in perfectly and he's on schedule because he bought in. It took a while. So he didn't want to come to huddle meetings. He'd say, "It's a waste of my time." He was like, "I only got three guys here, it's a waste of my time." I said, "You're getting buried because you're not coming to the meetings. You're not getting what you need because you're not communicating what you need." And he thought about it.

And he would always be calling them up. "Siri, call so-and so" every day. And I wouldn't give up on him. Some people said, "He's not worth it. Just bury him. This will make his life difficult." That's not a team, right? If we're all members of the team and we're all equal partners then why let your fellow team member suffer by not coming to the meeting, getting what he needs to be successful, communicating where he needs to work and where he can move for other people?

That's how I started out, but it didn't end like that. It took a while for him to speak up in that meeting. He told me after the meeting, "I'm not comfortable speaking in the group." I said, "If you're not comfortable with speaking in the group, you will not finish successfully on this project."

He asked what I meant and I said, "These guys will do anything for you if you will communicate it." I remember the first meeting where he spoke up and said, "Guys, I need to work in this area before you go in or you're going to bury me." The electrician said, "Oh, go ahead. I can wait till Wednesday. Can you finish that in two days?" I said, "Heck yeah," and he looked at me like, "Wow, that's all I had to do?"

From then on we had open communication with maps. On our board we have maps and pens and everything that can help communicate and draw visually where people need to be to be successful. If everything's designed and thin, it looks beautiful. The schedule looks pretty and beautiful, but you know when you get on-site, all the different layers of the mechanical systems, plumbing, and electrical—it gets more complicated. It takes teamwork, daily teamwork to make that happen.

I remember early in my career, I would run around a lot. I think I got fifty thousand steps a day just running left and right and solving problems. I loved it. Adrenaline all day. I'd go home tired, but I couldn't be there for my family because I was so worn out. I loved work. But with that meeting, it's taken thirty thousand steps and a lot of headache off my day as we meet together, talk about the roadblocks and create energy and teamwork. We're a family in there. We laugh a lot, and he laughs now.

Jason - I'm really just kinda geeking out listening to you because first of all, the people on the podcast can't see you like I can see you on the Zoom call. You smile when you talk about this.

So give me five things that you do that have really helped you accomplish this.

Ricky - Alright. I don't know how you lead a troop if you don't know who you're leading. Everyone has different personalities. I was talking to a trade partner and told him I was going to do this podcast and asked if he wanted me to share anything, and he said, "Well Ricky, you do a good job bringing people's personalities out." And if you bring out people's true personalities, if they can say whatever they think, that makes all the difference.

My thought is—let me hear it. Let me hear your frustration, let me hear your jokes, let me hear your snide remarks to me or anybody. I love it. Bring out the personalities. And when you let people be who they are, with all the different backgrounds, and you let that happen, it's comfortable, it's fun, and you can say anything to anybody in our huddles, and no one takes offense.

So, number one is to know who you lead. Everyone has a different trigger, everyone has a different goal. Some people want to make their boss look good, some people want to make money, some people want to work so hard that they can hunt in New Zealand all fall. As you get to know people, amazing things happen. These aren't just skilled professionals we work with, they're building America every day. It's just amazing that as a superintendent, as a project engineer, project manager, field engineer, we get to work with the professionals of the world. Pretty cool blessing there.

My second one is zero tolerance. People have always said, "Ricky, you're too nice." I ask, "What do you mean? You don't go to hell for being too nice, do you?" They say, "Well Ricky, you're too nice. How can you be a superintendent?"

"I don't know. That's what I want, that's what I want to do." I can still be nice and still hold people accountable, and smile, and love life while holding the line. We just had an OSHA visit on-site. Their rep drove around five times trying to catch us. We had a lot of people. We had a large tower almost 210 feet in the air, and the scaffolding is being erected, and everyone's tied off. She drove around five times trying to catch those people not being tied off.

She walked in the building, she walked the site, she was very impressed how clean it was, and she really wanted an issue type citation. She told me this after the walk. She walks in, it's gorgeously clean and everyone's wearing their mask and everyone was safe, and we didn't get any citations that day. It was amazing.

So zero tolerance is key and what you are going to put up with. And you don't have to be a jerk about zero tolerance. You can be nice and happy and hold people accountable, but you have to be consistent. For your own self-perform craft, you can't turn back to them and let them do what they want to do, but then you hold everyone accountable.

You can't let your friends get away with anything. You gotta be 100% accountable for everything with zero tolerance. Safety and cleanliness. If you start there, you'll have a successful project and you'll be safe and you will have an enjoyable time as you build America together.

Jason - I love that. That's two. Third one...

Ricky - Third... so I talked about meeting with foremen, but meeting as a job in a worker huddle—that's a big thing too. Because people will think, "Who's this arrogant prick who walks the job and holds everyone accountable? Who's this guy?" I thought, well, let them see the real you. Get out and talk to people. But as you meet as a whole team, all two hundred workers spaced six feet apart with a microphone talking about the wins and some of the losses of the week, and having the owner's rep there, communicating how awesome everyone's doing, how pleased the community is, and how clean and organized, and how everything's safe on-site...that will change minds and build a culture.

We have to remember we're dealing with professionals, we aren't dealing with amateurs. This is a big deal. So as you treat people as professionals, and not amateurs, they will rise to the occasion or they're already there. We treat people like professionals. Like in Major League Baseball, you don't see the attitude, "Okay, this guy is not very good, so we're going to screw it up and we're going to throw him an underhand pitch. Because he's not very good, he can't handle the standards of a professional."

When we weaken him, we don't make him feel like an all-star. We don't make them feel like a professional. We can hold people accountable and they will rise to that accountability, to the new standard of construction. Because construction is getting tough. We're getting less and less trained craft in the field, which is amazing for the craft. They'll get paid more and more because they have a trade that no one else has, and that's an amazing thing.

So, as we hold people accountable, they will rise to the standards or to your vision. And as a superintendent, that's a great blessing because you can share your vision. You don't have to tell everyone how to get there, you share your vision and other people will catch the vision and hold others accountable.

It's amazing to walk the project and other trades are holding other trades accountable, not just for safety, not just for cleanliness, but for quality. They call each other out. What projects do you know where people can call out each other without fighting? Well, I haven't been on too many of them, but they can. Because we're all in this together.

Ricky - Our fourth key indicator is how we treat people. I've been on projects when the design team and the contractors just bad talk each other, back and forth, back and forth. Why? If we're on the same team, we've got to work together. We've got to work things out professionally, because they're on our team. We're all one team, fighting waste and variation.

If we can eliminate those two things from our industry, everyone's goals will be accomplished. Everyone will get paid more. They'll be happier, their home life will be better, and they will be winners because they will feel like they're professionals contributing to America and making it great.

My favorite thing about construction is the people. Some people... Let me share a quick story about this. I've worked for the number one contractor in the world for revenue, business. It's a big company. They had their in-house engineers, and I got to be pretty good friends with this one engineer—great beautiful mind, great intelligent man.

I was talking to him, asking why he was so antisocial because he had a beautiful mind and many things to share. And he says, "Ricky...I laugh thinking about it. He said, "Ricky, I'm not antisocial. I just don't like people."

How sad is that? And I think that's my reason why construction is amazing, because I love people. I seriously love people and I love hearing their stories, I love hearing their struggles. I love to hear where they've been. In our industry, we have a lot of people who speak Spanish and I've been blessed to speak Spanish, so when I walk a job, I speak a lot of Spanish.

It creates a bond right there, right off. I can ask questions about your family and your past and where you're going, and how vacation was and how the weekend was. And as we get to know people, we really get to know their needs, and we can address those needs as leaders. That might sound too touchy-feely, but it's working and I'm enjoying it.

Jason - I think that it's...no, I don't think...I know that it's what we needed to hear today. Because something that I just learned is that sometimes people have difficulty with the systems that we talk about. I've been wondering why some folks have difficulty and others...it's a natural fit. And I don't know that it has everything to do with personality. Some personalities tend more towards the people side of things, but there's a huge difference between a superintendent who cares about people and one who is just there to maybe escape or run away or just there for the job.

I think the moment we need to capture here is that we really don't lead construction, we really don't lead technical stuff, we build people. The superintendent is not a builder of things. The superintendent's not a builder of materials only and is not a builder of processes. More than anything, a superintendent is a builder of people.

And so what I've learned just in this little interview is that builders will be successful with the systems that we advocate, whether it's zero tolerance or whether it's nothing hits the ground, cleanliness first, quality at the source, whatever we're doing. If they care about people, then they will work through people and work through teams to get that done.

Ricky - Yeah, and the crazy thing with the human experience is people can really know. You can't fake like you care. Try it. You just can't feel it. I've seen people do that in their career, try to use people to hit their own goals in their career. The company I work for now just created a marvelous scene where you're not competing against the guy next to you. We're all a team. We all have the same goals. It's a team effort. We're not competing against each other.

Jason - The vision for this would be that we see that scaling up excellence, and there's actually a book about that, it's absolutely fantastic that our leadership will go so much further and go so much better as we give. And I encourage you and Ricky encourages you too, to read the book, The Go-Giver by Bob Burg and John David Mann.

Go be the person that you want to be and leverage people and teams to build these projects because we really don't build great things, we build great people first who build great things. So the vision for this would be for us to really share, to be successful, and to take it to the next level.

So until we meet again, may God bless your journey. Hopefully you'll catch the vision. Please go do something that betters the environment, betters people. Make that connection. Do something that inspires you. Do something that is similar to the moment when Ricky brought me up to one of the upper rooms in this religious facility, a room that's quite special to him, where he said, "Get over here," and gave me a quick hug. He said, "Do you feel that? You feel that right there?" And just feel the love of construction, love of people, the excitement for what we're doing, and the fact that we're going to make a difference. And so let's get it done, guys. On we go. –End of transcript--

We should all be able to learn from Ricky. The superintendent is not just the driving force of the project. He or she is the one who builds the team that will drive it. First, figure out who to bring on the bus, then get everyone in the right seats, and then figure out where to drive the bus. Team balance and health is the first and most important consideration when building a project. The second major topic of this book is to focus on you. How can you show up and be successful as a part of the team? What does it take? How do you do it? Glad you asked. We will now focus on…

THE ART OF THE BUILDER

Part 2 - The Leader

Being a senior or general superintendent does not mean you have reached a tenured level of authority. It means you have reached a level where you work through other people. It means you must model and encourage certain behaviors that are successful. You are now a coach, a mentor, and a manager. To do this you must be familiar with some key concepts. I will explain these briefly, one by one:

1. Success habits - These are the habits that make great leaders and top performers. This pattern is taken from Brendan Berchard's book, *High Performance Habits*. Following these habits will bring you to a level where you can properly lead your teams. Without them, you may not be playing on a level high enough to elevate and lead others.

2. Success formula - This success formula has been used by many top performing construction leaders with much success. If the habits help you to perform, the success formula directs that performance so you reach your goals and the goals of the team. Without the success formula, you may be a top performer going nowhere.

3. The characteristics of generals - There are certain characteristics that make for a great leader and superintendent. Characteristics like transparency and

vulnerability are key here. Why? Because we need to create vulnerable and transparent environments, and how goes the leader, so goes the job. We work on ourselves first. In this section I will cover key characteristics every senior leader must have. Without them, your job will be blocked or capped at the level of your performance wherever that may be.

4. Blocks to leadership - Even the best leaders have impediments that hold them back and cap their progress. As someone the project needs, and as someone who has so much influence and potential to do good, it would do you well to overcome these impediments. Blockages are the things that prevent you from doing what you need to do—build the team, have hard conversations, manage direct reports, hold remarkable meetings, and scaling clarity. If something is holding you back from doing those things, it must be removed. This section lists out the most common blocks to leaders in your role. If you break through, you can go as far as you want. If you do not, you will go only as far as your fears will let you.

5. The 7 deadly sins - In doing a small study of what holds superintendents back, I found a pattern of unlearned skills that would predict and stall someone's career. They usually show up anytime a super gets bogged down. If you reflect and take the time to learn these skills, you will be blessed. If not, you may be damned to stay in your current role forever.

In summary, our first task is to build a successful leader. Our second step is to get that leader doing the right things at the right times. Our third step is to get that leader doing the right things at the right time and in the right way. And lastly, we want that leader not to be held back by any mental block or unlearned habit. This is going to be remarkable. Get ready. You now know how to build a team. Can you build yourself?

Success Habits - (Developing The Leaders of This Journey)

Habit 1 - Gaining Clarity

There is a general approach I have used on multiple projects that will allow any project leader, project superintendent, senior superintendent, or general superintendent to be successful. Additionally, if you teach other superintendents that you're mentoring this approach, they will be successful as well. The outline goes as follows: First, we must gain clarity on what we're doing in our own role and for the project. Second, we need to develop the energy and motivation to accomplish it. Third, we need to create the necessity and sense of urgency to keep everybody in a time rhythm. Fourth, we need to increase productivity and find a way to create flow in all aspects of the work and throughout the project team. Fifth, we need to develop influence. This is key not only in assembling and building the team, but in perpetuating a team that will be successful on a construction project. Finally, having courage is one of your main roles as a construction leader in order for you to be successful.

I will admit that this pattern was something that I followed throughout my career, but distilling it down to these few words is something that I stole from Brendon Burchard's *High Performance Habits*. I feel they apply nicely to this book and to the successful approach any senior level superintendent can take.

First, gaining clarity. The approach to take when you're gaining clarity is to know what the project encapsulates and who you have to be to accomplish it. You cannot tackle every project the same way. You need to understand what the project needs, design the approach, and then tailor both you and your approach to fit that construction project perfectly. I remember reading in General George S. Patton's biography that he literally designed the war hero that he became. His language, style of pistol, the way he wore his uniform, the way he fought and acted, the fact that he would always wear his helmet, his approach, his philosophy—all of these concepts were designed; none were accidental, all were intentional.

You, as a construction general, must do the same. Ask yourself, what does this project mean? How will I build it? Get a general sense of it as if you were a military general assessing the terrain and/or opponent and then devise the ideal person to build it. That is the kind of clarity you need to create. The ability to do so will manifest itself as you create your Leader Standard Work and your resolutions.

During my time at a research laboratory, I gave this idea a lot of thought. I looked at that one hundred million dollar project and its location in relation to my eventual move to Tucson, Arizona, and I started to contemplate the person who would build it. What would my Weekly Standard Work look like? What would my resolutions and behavior need to be to fill that role? What would my patterns need to be on a weekly basis in order to accomplish this? And then, what systems would I use in my to-do list, my email, my Outlook, my communication systems? I tried to leave no stone unturned in my thought process. What would my truck look like? What would my desk look like? What would my home office look like? What would my path home look like? Everything was designed to accommodate the project and the role.

I examined the needs I would have to become the kind of person I needed to become in relation to my location. Contemplation brought clarity and I was able to determine the following:

- I knew exactly what it was going to take to build that project.
- I knew what team was going to build that project;
- I knew where I was going to live in relation to the staging areas and offices for the project.
- I designed my transportation systems traveling from Phoenix to Tucson to accommodate my schedule.
- I designed my desk area and my space and all of my computer and Internet systems to where I could build the project successfully.
- I created a Leader Standard Work system where the meeting system and all of my standard leader habits were custom-tailored in a way that I could fulfill my role perfectly in that role as a senior superintendent.
- I made sure that my resolutions, my personal resolutions and any personal documents that reminded me of who I was to be and who I was becoming on a daily basis, and my morning routine, aligned me so that I could be the right leader for what I was doing.

I literally designed the person I wanted to become for that construction project and I have continued to do it for every project, every situation, and every role change that I have ever encountered throughout my career. My challenge to you is to meticulously anticipate your scenarios on a wide scope to achieve clarity and design the person that will absolutely win on that construction project without fail. Once you have clarity, you will begin...

Habit 2 - Developing Energy

Developing energy is the next step in the process of making sure you are ready to approach and win with the construction project. Energy can come from a number of different sources that can include mental and physical health, proper motivation, and having less friction throughout life and in your circumstances. Developing energy is a key focus because it takes a lot of energy to lead a team and a lot of energy within that team to lead a project. You are not paid for your knowledge alone; you are also paid for the spirit in which you implement what you know.

I remember nearing the end of a two-year project and it was becoming obvious there was a certain amount of fatigue amid the ranks. Work had slowed, and there wasn't any sense of enthusiasm to get to the finish line. My morning huddles began to include passionate speeches throughout the next few weeks to re-energize and build motivation.

As we were doing our team reflections at the end of the project, the project manager spoke up and commented on my energy level and how it kept everyone on track. He credited me with giving the team the drive we needed to finish. I appreciated his words because it made me realize how important it is for a leader to provide that energy. I learned how imperative it is for a leader to act in ways that improves the energy and keeps it flowing. Eating properly and having an exercise routine was crucial for me. I remember key times when building certain projects, especially when I was working in Tucson, when I would travel back and forth for long distances. Sometimes I did not feel like I had the brain capacity to listen to books and take in any new information because I was in a cognitive decline. I had allowed myself to get too distracted and too busy at work. I wasn't working out and I wasn't eating right.

Challenging myself was difficult, but I made the effort to get back on track with my jogging routine and made healthier food choices. I could almost immediately tell that these small changes improved my mental capacity and gave me the energy to focus on the projects and things I needed to do.

I would also create playlists on my Apple Music that provided motivation and animation for me, and I would listen to those songs in the morning as I approached the project site so that my shoulders could be back, my head could be up, and my body could be alert and ready to go in the right physical, emotional, and mental state. For me, finding the proper motivation remains an essential part of my success.

Be aware of your waning energy and find your best way to recover. Design your energy as an intentional, integral part of your approach to constructing your project. You will need that energy when...

Habit 3 - Creating Necessity

The next step in the general process for a construction senior superintendent or general to follow is to create necessity and to have a sense of urgency. As we talked about at the beginning of this book, a team has to have a multiplier leader, the five key behaviors that every team needs to succeed, and a strenuous performance goal. It is the general's responsibility to have a sense of vision and purpose to create that drive, urgency and necessity. The senior super must have a master schedule that shows design, permitting, coordination, procurement, the targeted NTP, mobilization, foundations, superstructure, interiors/exterior, commissioning, site work, and all remaining features of the building as it ties into final inspections and deadlines on the project. The lead superintendent must understand what a temporary certificate of occupancy means, what substantial completion means, what it takes to receive a certificate of occupancy, and what the final stages in the project will entail and how difficult they will be. As soon as this happens, the leader will understand the key milestones and start to drive with a sense of urgency.

Most people will have a mental picture of project milestones six to twelve weeks behind of when they should be. It is your role as the lead superintendent on the project to understand the true scenario and create the drive and sense of urgency to motivate the entire team to revise their mental images of the schedule. To quote from *The Art of War* by Sun Tzu, "Put them on death ground," which is a war strategy that suggests the leader should back up the army against a river or a mountain to create a sense of urgency and necessity so that they fight like lions in the proper direction. We need this same urgency on our projects if we are going to fight like lions to complete our projects.

A superintendent does this same thing for the workforce and the project team. They must be on death ground. They must know exactly when the milestones are and anticipate every possible outcome. Urgency and necessity are part of the psyche of the lead superintendent from day one. It is your job and your job alone. If you don't feel it then you should find a way to obtain it so you can drive people forward in a proper manner. Not push-drive.

When I was first putting together the plan for the research laboratory, we had a twenty month schedule. The overall project scope increased by adding one floor. When I included that information by using a Takt plan, we realized as a project team it would take twenty-three and a half months. The way the project needed to be built, according to owner requirements, meant that it had to be fully functional by the end deadline which meant that in a complex laboratory, all of the systems had to be up and running from a commissioning standpoint with final balancing and final flush on the substantial completion day. Commissioning activities and any key startup had to move forward by a minimum of eight weeks from where it originally needed to be done.

Additionally, the air handlers needed to be done and up and running ahead of the hot summer months and monsoon season in the region. And so those key milestones necessitated a string of activities that worked all the way back to the initial electrical upgrades that happened in the existing basement of the adjacent building and necessitated us moving the work to be early. I don't mean pushing and rushing. I mean driving early procurement for the electrical equipment, the switch gear, and the planning of all of our infrastructure and working at a steady and safe pace. From day one, I was driving those activities so we could eventually accomplish the commissioning. There was a superintendent who was building a similar sized building next to me who did not do that, and they finished twelve months later because they did not consider the urgency and the necessity surrounding the milestones and the sequence with which the building had to be completed.

You must challenge yourself to see the overall picture, anticipate future outcomes, and to see things that other people do not see. Make it your purpose to create the rhythm, the urgency, and the speed at which the entire team should perform their activities so they can hit the targets and accomplish the milestones. You must have urgency. With that urgency, we must begin...

Habit 4 - Increasing Productivity

Throughout this book, we discuss how to increase team, individual, and crew productivity, but this general principle applies for all of us at a macro level. Your role is to increase the productivity levels of everyone on your project site. During the early stages of a key project in Arizona, the team was spread throughout the state. We were quite a distance away from one another and team members had different office set-ups with varying degrees of Internet. This wasn't very productive from a communication standpoint. My solution was to order two or three mobile minis to be brought to the project site so we could gather everybody together and increase proximity and communication. We set these up with temporary power in an urgent manner. We did not have the project trailers up and running, but we mobilized the team immediately in order to create that synergy and the throughput of information which increased our productivity. We began working like a team and brought that project out of the ground on schedule. The project executive validated my actions further when he told me that my mentality was crucial to getting out of the ground and that we couldn't have done it without that sense of urgency and without increasing the productivity of the team.

So many teams wait and do not gather to create that proximity and increased communication, and they suffer for it. They are not being as productive as they possibly could be. Remember, it is your responsibility to make sure you structure things so the team can be productive. That is true for the project team, the trade partners, the trade foremen, and everyone on-site. But it is most especially true for you. Set up the systems that allow you to be the most productive. There is no virtue or humility in sacrificing your own productivity. If you, as the lead superintendent, need a considerable amount of wall space, two or three desks, a special plan table, certain technology, additional screens, or an environment where you can see better with greater productivity, you need to get those things regardless of whether you have the budget for it. You have to make sure that your own productivity as a leader and the productivity as a team is priority number one and two. So if you have to get that extra desk, get it. If you have to order that screen, order it. If you have to upgrade that computer, do it. If you need to buy that iPad, buy it. If you need a closer parking stall so you can save fifteen minutes in the morning and allow you additional planning time, make it happen. You need to create circumstances to increase your productivity and the productivity of the team. You can help others with their productivity when you begin...

Habit 5 - Developing Influence

Influence is something that is crucial for any leader in any realm of business, but it is absolutely crucial as the lead role on the construction project site. When we were about to build the research laboratory, I stacked the deck in my favor in the assembly of the project team by hiring three key positions: senior project engineer, systems superintendent, and field engineer. These were people with whom I already had a certain amount of trust and rapport and I was certain they would help create a cohesive team even before we began the project.

After those initial hires we quickly worked together as a team to gain influence with everyone and to build the team first. The project executive and the project manager immediately began encouraging us to copy each other on emails, to have weekly team meetings, to do team building events, to do personality assessments, and to have interpersonal conflict that allowed us to have influence with one another. This was a key strategy from the beginning, and one of the main reasons that we were wildly successful.

You may not have the opportunity to gain influence by stacking the deck in hiring key positions on your project, but you can begin immediately developing influence with other people throughout your organization, people who could be on future projects.

You must start to develop influence with the people who are on your projects and win them over. This is the only way. If you do this, you will be able to move your ideas forward in a way so they can be implemented. Once you have influence within the team and the company, you must immediately begin to build influence with trade partners, trade foremen and everyone else on-site including the vendors and the owner to leverage and implement ideas throughout the construction project. With this influence, you will be the great leader you need to be by forging ahead and...

Habit 6 - Having Courage

Every great leader must have the courage to implement their ideas. Knowledge is not power; action is power.

During the closing out of one of our projects, owner representatives and corporate leaders were getting nervous about whether or not we were going to finish on time and they recommended adding manpower and increasing crews. They began to push in a frantic way outside of clean, safe, organized and stable methods. As the lead senior superintendent on that project site, I remember holding them back and drawing a very strict line on the way we were going to finish evenly and smoothly down to the project finish. Thirty percent of the project had been changed by design change orders and other types of change orders throughout the project, and there was a lot that still needed to be managed and accomplished as a team in order to finish on time.

It took courage to hold everybody accountable to maintaining a clean, safe, and organized project in a smooth and steady flow. I remember a caravan of people from corporate coming down to do fresh eyes reviews of the project every month. They would ask us to begin pushing, and every month I held them back. We evaluated where the team was, gave them a snapshot, listened to their feedback, and told them that the project was going to finish in a clean, safe, stable environment, and that we would keep consistent crew levels and crew composition. There was a little bit of a push back for sure, but the project manager and I made it clear enough that they backed off. We ended up finishing that project down to the day in a remarkable fashion, and we did it the entire time while being clean, safe and organized.

If you are going to be the lead senior superintendent on your project site, you must lead with courage. Everybody must be held accountable, and no plan, theory, concept, strategy, or tactic—logistical or otherwise—can be implemented without it. Ultimately courage and the ability to hold people accountable is one of the single most value add attributes of a senior superintendent. I remember implementing certain progressive logistics, improved trailer complexes, new crane types, adjusted working hours, new scheduling systems like Takt plans, and massive efforts like room kitting and pre-fabrication. But ultimately, if the project success is on me, then I am going to make sure I find the courage to execute the strategies and tactics I know will ensure timely productivity, progress, and profit.

If you're going to be a successful project leader, you must have a remarkable amount of courage every step of the way.

Zero tolerance cannot be implemented without courage, safety rules cannot be implemented without courage, perfect cleanliness cannot be implemented without courage, stable logistics systems cannot be implemented without courage, schedules and holding the schedule milestones cannot be implemented without courage.

The Success Formula - (Doing The Right Things at The Right Time)

Ingredient 1 - Clarity

There is another pattern for successful leaders, which I call the success formula. The main points for this formula are clarity, mindset, personal organization, and a morning routine. These are the habits that great leaders will follow and thread throughout their lives in order to be successful. First, a great construction leader must have clarity, on not only what they're doing, but where they want to go in their career, and most especially what they want in life. Second, that leader must have the right mindset. He or she must have a rich mindset and a growth mindset to be successful. Third, that leader must be personally organized and have a remarkable personal organization system. And finally (and this is a very important part) that leader must have a morning routine to center her or himself every day on the concepts of giving and gratitude and to focus on the things which will make him or her the most successful.

Clarity. This is different from the previous section. Every leader must have clarity on who they want to be and where they want to go. In reflecting back on my own life, I remember an occasion when I went on a boy scout trip with other youth leaders. While the kiddos were in merit badge courses, I had the time to read through a book called *Unbeatable Mind: Forge Resiliency and Mental Toughness to Succeed at an Elite Level* by Mark Divine. That book challenged me to design my future life so I could look back on it with pride rather than a slough of wasted effort. The author asked if I knew my true purpose. At that time I was also reading a book by Dave Ramsey called *EntreLeadership; 20 Years of Practical Business Wisdom from the Trenches*, and in that book, he recommended creating a vision statement which included your purpose, mission, and core values to make sure that you're centered and anchored on those key concepts.

I combined ideas from both those books to create a clarity statement for myself, and began to craft what became a decade-long journey that revealed my desire to be a teacher. My core values were centered on building and protecting people and families, and I also realized I wanted to be the Tony Robbins of construction and really elevate the industry. This little exercise, this focus on gaining clarity about my personal life really enabled me to shape the rest of my life and do things in each of my individual roles that has made me feel as successful as I possibly can be. I have progressed rapidly towards my goals in every role because of that clarity.

The crucial steps to gaining clarity are:

1. Create your vision. This will consist of your mission, purpose, and values.

    a. Your mission outlines what you are going to accomplish before you pass away.

    b. Your purpose statement explains why that mission is important.

    c. Your core values are the things that you value as a human being. Values that you would not violate or go against under any circumstances.

2. Once you have your vision you will identify what is most important for you right now. What next step do

you need to take in the next six to eighteen months to eventually accomplish your mission?

3. This immediate, or thematic goal as Patrick Lencioni calls it, will help you to create at least five specific defining goals. These are the goals that will help you accomplish your thematic goal. They are the specifics, the small steps.

Here is a quick example.

Mission - To oversee field operations in my company by the age of 65, completely develop a training program for all positions, and leave the company with one of the best field development programs in the industry.

Purpose - My purpose is to create lasting change in the construction industry by elevating the field operations in the company I currently work for.

Core Values - Family, God, good friends, excellent work, and dedication are what is most important to me.

Thematic Goal - Be ready to become a senior superintendent in eighteen months.

Defining Goal #1 - Mentor my on-site supers to function without me and replace me as project superintendent within twelve months.

Defining Goal #2 - Begin adding value with preconstruction efforts to prove my value in project development and setup. Gain the trust of company leadership with pre-con within ten months.

Defining Goal #3 - Take advanced scheduling training to learn Takt planning, Last Planner®, and Scrum to fully augment my planning abilities within sixteen months.

Defining Goal #4 - Tour another project every month to add value, learn from others, and develop influence in my business unit.

Defining Goal #5 - Lose twenty pounds by eating healthy, working out, and getting enough sleep before the eighteen month deadline.

Hopefully you can see how the mission, the purpose, the values, your thematic goal, and your defining goals all tie together to form a complete picture of where you want to go. Everyone should have this. It will literally guide every footstep you take in your career. If you do not know where you are going, how to get there, and what is most important right now, you are likely wasting time and life. Now that you know this, what will you do next?

Ingredient 2 - Mindset

Mindset is crucial and will literally determine all your success in life. Think about this: If you make a certain amount of money, it is because your mind is programmed to make that much. If you have a certain type of marriage, it is because your mindset is programmed to have that kind of marriage. If your project is dirty, it is because your mind is dirty. If your projects are behind schedule, it is because you are a behind-schedule-mindsetted person. Everything comes down to mindset. I am not making any assumptions about how you obtained your mindset. It could have come from nature or nurture or both. My point is that there are obtainable mindsets that are cleaner, safer, more profitable, happier, and more productive. If you want a different mindset than what you have, find a mentor, a coach, training, or an experience that will model the mindset you want. Through repetition, you will be able to shape your mindset to bring you the success you desire. There are two really important ones for us in construction: growth versus fixed and rich versus poor. Let me briefly explain these here...

Growth versus Fixed

Growth:

A growth mindset defines success as growth and improvement. When we choose to have this mindset we work hard from a passion for learning and excellence. This mindset leads to winning as a by-product of constantly growing and improving. This mindset, when held, will enable you to...

1. Focus on learning, not being validated.
2. Seek challenges in spite of fear.
3. Search for ongoing improvement as a way of life.
4. Grow from failure and fail forward.
5. Accept effort as a key to success.
6. Celebrate the success of others instead of being jealous.

This mindset defines success by how much we are growing, not by how much we know.

These are also the people that become multiplier leaders.

Fixed:

When we have a fixed mindset we define success as being error-free, smart, or right. It is a mindset focused on having instead of becoming. This mindset may lead to working hard for a success symbol or status, but has a very hard time breaking through to the next level once that status is reached. When we drift into this mindset, we...

1. Focus on validation.
2. Seek certainty.
3. Prejudge the potential of others.

4. Crack under pressure or perceived failure.
5. Become reluctant to put in extra effort because of a fear of failure.
6. Become jealous or feel threatened by the success of others.

This mindset defines success by how much we know, are acknowledged, and how smart and special we perceive ourselves to be. This leads to misery and a lack of fulfillment.

These are also the people who become diminishing leaders unless they choose to change.

This is covered extensively in the book *Mindset: The New Psychology of Success* by Carol Dewek.

Wealthy vs. Poor

Wealth:
Being wealthy doesn't just mean having money, but I will say that being able to manage money and wealth will help the other categories of wealth in life. People who say money doesn't buy happiness are shopping in the wrong stores. To be great, you must lean into adopting a wealthy mindset.

- Success is an obligation. People who are wealthy with money and life believe they are obligated to be successful so they can help others.
- I must take responsibility for my future. Wealthy people take responsibility for their own future, their own career, and do not leave it to company leaders or company 401k plans.
- I invest money. Wealthy people invest money so their money is working for them.
- I am continuously learning. Wealthy people in money and mind are constantly learning, reading, and paying for training, coaching, and mentoring.

- I focus on future opportunities. Wealthy people look to future opportunities and act when others do not.
- I am net-worth driven. Wealthy people focus on their net worth, not just what is in savings or the bank account. They have a healthy overall view of wealth and wealth strategy.
- I think big. Wealth building people think big.
- I embrace change. Wealthy people embrace change even when it is hard.
- I solve problems. Wealthy people solve problems instead of just accepting them as normal.
- I have multiple streams of income. Wealthy people have multiple sources of income and diversify.
- I am goal driven. Wealthy people set goals beyond their current capabilities so they can grow.

<u>Poor:</u>

You cannot give food from an empty pantry. You cannot loan money from an empty bank account. You cannot give advice from an empty mind. Being poor is not bad. Being content to remain empty is selfish. We gain so we can give. You cannot be a giver if you have nothing to give.

- Success is unimportant. People who are poor do not feel an obligation to others to become rich because they do not feel an obligation to give.
- I blame others. Poor people blame others and play the victim. They let others determine their future and their future wealth.
- I spend my money. Poor people spend all their money and live week to week.
- I refuse to learn to my potential. Poor people become poor in mind because they refuse to learn.

- I focus on the past. Poor people live in the past and miss opportunities for the future.
- I am income-driven. Poor people are income driven and do not invite other sources of income.
- I think small. Poor people think small so they do not have to feel small in their efforts.
- I fear change. Poor people let fear keep them from being nimble, adapting, and changing.
- I focus on problems. Poor people focus on problems and let that become their reality.

This is covered extensively in the book *Secrets of the Millionaire Mind: Mastering the Inner Game of Wealth* by T. Harv Eker.

Your personal clarity will not matter one bit if you have the wrong mindset. You can be headed in a certain direction, but if you cannot grow into that direction and if you cannot have a mindset of abundance and wealth, you will fail along the way. These tie directly together. Mindsets are there for the taking. My mentor, coach, and trainer is Tony Robbins. I spend time annually participating in his events, training, and coaching programs so I can expand my mindset and influence. The key is to ask yourself where you want to improve. Do you have a rich mindset? If not, which method will help you improve? Now that you know this, what will you do now?

Ingredient 3 - Personal Organization

You will go nowhere without a personal organization system so I encourage you to take this seriously. In the book *Elevating Construction Superintendents*, I suggested keeping a to-do list; however, that is only part of what's needed. I suggest the following:

- To-Do List - Write everything down in one location.

- Leader Standard Work - Have a plan for standard work that only you should do and only you can do.
- Weekly Planning - Plan every week ahead-of-time to maximize your life, your career, and your influence.
- Time Blocking - Merge your to-do list and weekly work plan and time block your day every day.
- Protecting Your Plan - Protect your plan to achieve success over sixty percent of the time or more.
- Tracking Progress - Track to ensure you achieve that sixty percent and make corrections and adjustments if you are not.

This is a guaranteed way to succeed. If you do not currently have a personal organization system, and you implement this with your whole heart, might, mind, and strength, you will achieve more success and fulfillment in the next five years than you could possibly imagine. If you don't believe me, try it, and give me a call in three to five years. That's my personal challenge to you. I have studied many books about personal productivity and have distilled this process down to what is necessary for the construction professional. So let's begin. Here is how it works:

Your To-Do List:
- Your mind is for having ideas, not holding them. Do not try to remember things you should be doing. When I see someone in construction not writing things down, I automatically know they have no idea what they are doing.
- You may have heard on social media or other books that to-do lists are unhealthy and ineffective. These are shock and awe campaigns. Do not believe them. You cannot be successful without a successful to-do list system.

- Quite a bit of your current unhealthy stress, anxiety, or depression could be because you are trying to remember things. You must imagine each item you try to remember like a pinball in your head. Until you remove it and put it on a to-do list or capturing system, it will ping around in your head, bruising the inner lining of your mind. Make no mistake. Much of your unhappiness at work and at home is due to an inadequate personal organization system.

To be effective, practice keeping a to-do list for at least sixty days straight which equates to about three months of working days. You can keep your to-do list on an app, in a field book, in a personal day timer, or a notepad. The method really doesn't matter. What matters is that it works for you. My favorites have been Microsoft To Do for online apps, Notes for Mac users, a personal day planner, or a regular old notepad with a sticky note for items you will do that day. Here is the idea though—everything that comes to you must be written down. This is called…

<u>Capturing</u>

Everything must be captured. Everything. Get it out of your head and onto a capture system. The measure of success with this is that you have a capturing system to reference throughout the day with little to no friction.

Include…
1. Ideas.
2. Action items.
3. What someone tells you to do.
4. What you are reminded to do.
5. What you volunteer for.
6. Anything from anywhere that you need to remember.

This information can come when...
1. In the shower.
2. Driving (please use voice commands for this).
3. Waking up.
4. Going to bed.
5. On vacation.
6. Having a quiet moment.
7. Taking a break.
8. You get sudden strokes of ideas.

Once you have captured your tasks, you must begin...

Clarifying

You need to clarify or discern what should be done and what should not be done. For this I will reference the method used by Dwight D. Eisenhower. General Eisenhower, who was instrumental in the Allied victory in World War II, used a matrix to determine what he would do and what he would not do. The vertical columns on the matrix were labeled urgent and not urgent. The horizontal rows were labeled important and not important. He would do right away the tasks that were at the intersection of important and urgent. The intersection of important and not urgent he would schedule much like we do today on Microsoft Outlook or Apple Calendar. The intersection of not important but urgent would be delegated to someone else, and the intersection of not important and not urgent he would delete from his list. This is a remarkable system. You can do it a number of ways, but the key to success is to do the things only you can and should do. Do not do what others can and should do. As educator and author Peter Drucker said, "There is nothing so useless as doing efficiently that which should not be done at all." Now that you know what you should do, you must begin...

Organizing

Once you know what you should be doing, organize each task into various buckets. You should have as few buckets as possible and those buckets should be accessible, useful, and addictive. For instance, when I was a superintendent, I would use my to-do list, meeting agendas, or Outlook. Once I knew I had a task, it would go on a program like Microsoft One Note, which I would bring up in a meeting, or to Outlook, as a schedule reminder or time blocked task. However you decide to organize, you must have buckets to capture what you have decided to do. Those buckets need to be visual, frictionless, addictive, and easily accessible. That will enable you to reference it throughout the day and...

Engage with Focus

Now that you have all your items captured, clarified, and organized, you should have a free mind to engage in your tasks. This is key. If you cannot fully focus on a task you will not be productive with it. There should be no other thoughts in your mind, distractions, or stresses. You need to give yourself over fully to that task and that task alone. You do not have the ability to multitask, and you're lying to yourself if you think you can. This concept is called one-piece flow in Lean thinking and I highly recommend it. Once you have completed your task you can then celebrate. You can feel accomplished and let your mind release reinforcing chemicals and hormones that create a habit loop out of finishing assignments, not just starting them.

And now we should talk about your...

Leader Standard Work:

I can make this quick for you. Twenty percent of what you do yields eighty percent of your return or benefit. Eighty percent of what you do only yields twenty percent of your return. This is a dismal thought, but it is true. Leader

Standard Work is the systematized protection of your twenty percent. And here is the fun part: Your clarity document is the finding of your twenty percent. Here is how this works: I want you to create a standard weekly calendar that shows what you, as a leader, must consistently do to be great. You will start with your dedication to God and your spirituality first. You will put in your time with family next. You will then plug in personal items needed to maintain good health and mental wellness. Next, you will plug in your standard work that only you can do and should do as a leader on your project. After that, plug in your five defining goals from your clarity document. Finally, plug in your standard meetings. Does this sound complex? Welcome to the world of being a superintendent. This is just how complex life is. I did not make the rules. It is your job to orchestrate a weekly calendar that allows you to have success spiritually, at home, with your health, your role, and the interactions you must have with others at work. A quick note here. You must follow that order. God first, family second, your well-being third, your role fourth, followed by your interactions with the team. If you run that backwards, you will never get past the chaos of the project.

The key to all this is that it's time blocked as a standard. The second key is for you to include your Clarity document goals. If your next milestone is to become a senior superintendent or general superintendent, and your five defining goals are to become proficient with Takt planning, assist your business unit with preconstruction, tour a project every month, mentor other superintendents, and become AGC CM-Lean certified, then those goals need to be scheduled in your Leader Standard Work. Here is an example of what I am talking about. Each of these goals can be transferred to a task on your weekly calendar.

- Become proficient with Takt planning - Schedule two hours to do training and update your schedule

- Assist your business unit with preconstruction - Schedule time every week to help review schedules or make them part of a pre-con effort
- Tour a project every month - Schedule time every fourth week for your job walk. Schedule time the first week to schedule the walk
- Mentor other superintendents - Schedule time to do a field walk with other supers to mentor and train them
- Become AGC CM-Lean certified - Schedule time every week to study the material ahead of your course

You would also see items like—

- Weekly family coaching
- Kid's baseball practice
- Date night with spouse
- Daily midday prayers

Your spiritual, family, personal, leader standard work, personal development, and meeting times are planned and happen as a matter of intention, not by accident. There is no merit to "trying" your best every week. You must plan it and execute based on that plan. What if your plan changes? It will. Remember, aim small, miss small. If you have a plan, you will accomplish more of it than you would if you did not have a plan. With this standard, you are ready to begin...

Weekly Planning:

Weekly planning is basically creating a weekly work plan for yourself. You have three different inputs for this—your scheduled activities for next week on Outlook, your Leader Standard Work, and your memory. Use all three of them and you can make a heck of a plan. If you use Outlook, you will make sure your standard Leader Standard Work items are plugged in. If you have PTO or something like a training or a one-off major activity, you will plan around those events to the best of your ability. As you go through next week's plan you will confirm or decline meetings and lock in all planned events and meetings so you can win in life and at work. The measure of success with this is that you can execute your plan for the next week and feel like you are successful with all or most aspects of your life. You should be able to engage in the plan with very little chaos. When I say plan, I mean daily...

Time Blocking:

Time blocking is when, on a daily basis, you merge your plan for the day with anything that may have recently come up on your to-do list. Take the top one, two, or five items from your to-do list that are urgent and important and see if they fit into your plan for the day—from the time you start your day and when you plan to finish it. If the items fit, you will time block them in with very little context switching and still leave yourself a twenty to forty percent buffer in case you get distracted with other important and urgent matters. Once you do this, you can follow your plan and live in day-tight compartments which will enable you to neither worry about the past nor the future. You can focus on the now and know that you are actually winning. But you will only be able to focus if you begin...

Protecting Your Plan:

There must be some common sense with this, but I will say you have to protect your plan. You will fiercely protect your plan as a default, but not at the expense of emergencies, key opportunities, and owner needs. You must be discerning. If a trade partner interrupts your focused task to ask you about an RFI, you will likely ask him to come back or do a little research before coming back. If there is a fire in the building or a major event that could derail the project, you will likely change tasks and focus where you are needed at the moment. The point is that you must be discerning. You protect when you can and adjust when you must. The measure of success is that you are able to accomplish over sixty percent of your planned work in a week. If you do, you will do more than ninety-nine percent of the rest of the population. Just get ready to expand your mindset because you are about to experience quite a bit of success—especially if you begin...

Tracking Progress:

If you really want to be successful with this system you will track your progress. In all the templates I make for Leader Standard Work and Clarity documents, I include a way to track progress. If you mark off what you were able and not able to accomplish, you can make adjustments that will serve you when creating future plans. This will translate to the bottom line in your life because you will constantly improve how well you implement this system. The measure of success is that you are able to see how well you are doing and make adjustments when improvements are needed. Remember, you cannot manage what you cannot measure, and you cannot measure what you cannot see.

I have been brief with the description of this system. If you want to fully implement this, I invite you to attend one of our Superintendent Boot Camps. If you want some quick reads to develop your own system, I recommend reading *Essentialism: The Disciplined Pursuit of Less* by Greg McKeown If you implement this you will progress beyond your imagination. If you do not, you can expect the same mediocre results you already have if you don't have your own system.

Ingredient 4 - Morning Routine

Now we get to the morning routine. This is the best part. To set this up I want to say that you should now understand that Clarity does little good without the right mindset. It should also be clear that someone with goals and mindset will not make it far without a personal organization system to implement their next steps to their goals on a daily basis. Additionally, all of it will be a waste of time without a morning routine. I will explain why.

Your morning routine is designed to reframe you into a grateful and giving mentality through neuro-associative conditioning. The plan is to condition your mindset to be grateful and to give back that day. It will change your actions from selfish, taking, grumpiness to a mindset of gratitude and a commitment to give to others. Without this, you might use your clarity, mindset, and personal organization system to take, use, exploit, and abuse others which results in leadership and environments that lack respect for people. But with it, you can aim all your efforts in a direction that will create true influence, by giving.

Here's how it works...

Let's start with what you do already. What do you do every morning that really works for you? Do you wake up, go jogging, make coffee, take a shower, or read the newspaper? Please make a list or think of this in your mind. I want you to take those actions and weave in two others—box breathing and your incantation.

Here is a typical example of what I find people typically do in their morning:
1. Wake up
2. Say prayers
3. Make coffee

4. Get dressed
5. Listen to a podcast on the way to work

Here is an example of a really intense morning routine I heard about:
1. Wake up
2. Say prayers
3. Drink water
4. Go jogging
5. Shower
6. Scripture time
7. Thinking time
8. Listen to book or podcast on the way to work

Whatever your routine is, it is important to remember that our routine shapes us. It's important to get it right and make it impactful. As you can see from my examples, there are different habits for different purposes. I would recommend the following at a minimum:

1. Spiritual aspect - This will frame morality and ethics into your mindset.
2. Physical aspect - Exercise invigorates the body.
3. Thinking aspect - Giving yourself time to think in the morning lets ideas come to you.

Now, to all of this, I would add box breathing and your incantation. To learn more about box breathing I highly recommend a book called *Unbeatable Mind: Forge Resiliency and Mental Toughness to Succeed at an Elite Level* by Mark Divine. Box breathing is a way to breathe while visualizing—and the visual part is important—a mental image of numbers as you make your way around a imaginary box. You breathe for twenty seconds—five second inhale, five second hold, five second exhale, and five second hold. Once you are done you have made it all the way around the box. As you breathe in, you imagine the numbers 1, 2, 3, 4, and 5 showing up in your mind. This does two things: The breathing creates focus, mindfulness, and regulates your heart rate while the focus on the numbers trains your mind in self-control. It really is quite remarkable. You do this while standing up, feet shoulder width apart with your head up and chest out. I suggest at a minimum to go three times around the box and to then put your hand over your heart and think about something you are truly grateful for. When you do that, really try to imagine that place. Go there in your mind and really feel it.

I recommend going a second three rounds in the box and then putting your hand over your heart asking the question "What will I do today to give to those around me?" You can breathe as long as you like and go around the box as many times as you like, but I have found that if you take this action daily for a minimum of sixty days, you can become a go-giver, be more grateful, and you will expand your influence as a leader dramatically. In the book *The Go-Giver: A Little Story About a Powerful Business Idea*, authors, John David Mann and Bob Burg, clearly show that giving leaders excel. This is what I want for you.

Additionally, do you remember the last time you were stressed about an idea you could not get rid of? Remember that time you were at church and you could not get rid of those inappropriate images in your mind? Remember the last time you were at home talking to your spouse when you could not shake the thought of anchor bolts or change orders or some mistake you made that day? Box breathing will help you get in control of that, reduce your bad stress, and let you focus and be present. It is quite remarkable. So, here is my personal recommendation for a great morning routine:

1. Wake up.
2. Write down any thoughts from the night before.
3. Do your religious or spiritual routine.
4. Exercise.
5. Do your box breathing routine—
   a. Box breathing
   b. Grateful thought
   c. Box breathing
   d. Giving thought
   e. Write down your thoughts to anchor them in
6. Shower. You will have some thinking time there. I suggest even having a waterproof notepad on the wall with a pencil.
7. On your way to work listen to something like a podcast or book.
8. Time block your day by merging your top to-do list items and your Leader Standard Work.
9. Have a great day and focus with as little context switching as possible.

The Characteristics of Generals - (Doing Things The Right Way)

If you become intentional and disciplined with success habits you will personally grow into a leader who can manage any reasonable size or number of projects. If you adopt the success formula you will direct those abilities toward project, career, and personal success by doing the right things at the right time. Now all you need is to do them the right way. This section has been written so you can use your success habits and the success formula in a manner that will maximize your influence and your personal fulfillment. You do not have to strive for the following characteristics, but you will pay the price if you do not. My recommendation would be to strive for these and to at least acknowledge their importance in your role as the leader of your project. First, you must be...

Focus 1 - Relatable

Introduction:

Every senior superintendent should work on becoming relatable to the people he or she leads. This is important because people must be able to find a connection and relate to their leaders in order to support their leaders. Ultimately, leadership only means that a person has the ability to influence others. Without being relatable, you cannot do this. There must be something that will build rapport with the team members, owner, designers, foreman, and workers in order for there to be a connection. This could be experience, similar skills, styles, approaches, or concern shown for other team members. Whatever you use, you must be relatable.

Story:

I remember a time when I was asked to spend a few hours with a project team to help them run their project. We discussed some aspects of the Integrated Production Control System at a high level and really only dove into a few key concepts. A key concept for me was to recommend that the team begin morning worker huddles to really create a cohesive culture and get everyone working together. They tolerated the idea as I presented it to them and later implemented it at the recommendation of the project director. I was surprised three weeks later when I returned to the project for a brief field walk to find out the huddles had not been successful. The workers and foremen were actually more disruptive and disconnected. They hated the senior superintendent on-site, and I was told the huddles were the cause of it. I was so surprised by this that I joined a morning worker huddle the next day. When I arrived I saw disengaged people, an impatient super, and a group of people who seemed to dislike each other. I was shocked to hear the senior super criticizing, talking down to, and talking at the workers and foremen in the huddle. He would say things like, "you guys," and "come on," and, "you will." I thought, "This guy is a jerk!" I knew why the huddles had not worked. He did not try to relate to the craft professionals and he did not attempt to establish a connection through rapport. I realized then that you cannot be an unrelatable a-hole and lead men and women in the field.

Unrelatable superintendents are targets, not team members.

Challenge and Application

I would challenge every superintendent who reads this book to first, learn to love the people on your project, second, attempt to establish rapport with them, and third, connect in meaningful ways. People do things for friends, not enemies. If you are an unreliable prick, you will not be able to fill the role of a senior superintendent because you will have influence with very few people. And without influence, you are not a leader. Now let's discuss having a...

Focus 2 - Good Character

Introduction:

Character is who you are, what you think, and how you act. Beliefs become actions, actions become habits, and habits become character. There is nothing that can help a senior supervisor more than morality, ethics and a good character. This is important because people on your projects will expect you to make ethical decisions, behave morally, do what you say you will do, and be fair. If you do not have this, you will lead the project in dangerous and risky directions.

Story:

I remember being on a project where I promised early on that there would be very few priority walls on levels 2, 3, and 4. The reason for this was the amount of overhead mechanical and plumbing that were required on those floors. In the basement and on level 1, the framer would not be able to get back into the interstitial space unless we framed a large number of priority walls. I put this in the schedule and the basis of the schedule so the project team could rally around the agreement. The plan was set. We exited preconstruction and began the project. Later on, the framing foreman, who was our foreman on our self-perform framing crew, asked if we could frame priority walls on all floors like we began in the basement and level 1. Without question, I told him no. Apparently this was not an acceptable answer because I was asked again and again until I said, "What do you not understand about this? We planned this together, made commitments, and cannot now screw another contractor out of time and money simply because it would benefit us." This also was not an acceptable answer because one of our company leaders that was over self-perform started driving two hours every week to visit our project and attend our self-perform meetings. That group reported that I was abusive and angry and that I should be removed. The leader found none of this to be true, asked one final time if we could change the plan, and I said no. Something that day stuck because we went forward with the plan and commitment we made to the other trade partners, but it was not without consequence. I remember being ridiculed, criticized, and maligned by people within my organization simply because I would not screw other contractors to make a dollar. At the end of all this the mechanical contractor PM complimented me for having integrity, making ethical decisions, and holding to what was right. I will also report that everyone made money in the end. I had to be the ethical and moral leader that was going to stand up and do what was right. It was disappointing that I had to go through this, but it was worth it.

Senior superintendents do what they say they will do, are fair to everyone on-site, and never ask anyone to do anything that is immoral and unethical.

Application and Challenge:

A superintendent will be asked or encouraged to do unethical and immoral things during the course of a project. That is a mathematical certainty. I would challenge you right now to make decisions that will support you later. You cannot successfully decide in the moment to do the right thing. It must be something you've already anticipated and decided. And when the time comes that you must hold your ground and stand alone, stand there tall and strong and be an example of doing what is right and standing for what is right. When you do this, you will influence others and become...

Focus 3 - A Mentor

Introduction:

Mentoring can be difficult, but it is crucial to the role of a senior superintendent. The role of a senior super transitions from leading and doing to leading and mentoring. There will be very few things that you get to actually, "do" in the course of your day. You will spend most of your time teaching, managing, correcting, coaching, and yes, mentoring the people on the team so they can do the doing.

Story:

I worked with a general superintendent in El Paso, Texas, who invited me to his project to do some field engineer training. The project was large and spread out on a federal military base. I noted he spent time with every person on the project team on a daily basis and did very little work as far as I could see. I asked him how such a large project was run so well and he told me, "Jason, I do not spend time doing things on a daily basis. I spend time with each person on the project and mentor them so they can do it. I am in the business of building people nowadays, not projects." What he said resonated with me and I have remembered it ever since.

Senior superintendents build people who build projects.

Application and Challenge:

That general superintendent in El Paso was right. A great leader will spend his or her time with other people. If you are in a senior role or wish to be in a senior role, you must become a supportive mentor to the other superintendents on and off your project. Not only is this how great companies are built, it is how you will grow and gain influence in your role. I recommend you schedule field walks, lunches, sit downs, and training time with all of your direct reports immediately. You may feel this is presumptuous and perhaps unnecessary, but I assure you that your people want this. I have trained thousands of people and I have never encountered a person who wanted to be left alone to figure things out on their own. Everyone I have ever asked about this topic wants facetime, coaching, mentoring, and management from their leaders—that includes you. Let's give it to them by being a mentor. You will thrive in this role as you open your mouth and also become a...

Focus 4 - A Communicator

Introduction:

There is nothing as useless as a senior superintendent who does not communicate. It is akin to hiring a lifeguard who doesn't swim. The main role of a senior superintendent is to lead with vision, align the project plan and schedule, and communicate that clarity to all parties on the project site so team members can see as a group, act as a group, and know as a group. If the senior super does not communicate and communicate well, he or she is not doing his or her job. Period.

Story:

I remember a superintendent who did not like to communicate. I will tell a different variation of this story later, but suffice it to say that he was a horrible communicator and did not want to lead his project. I was called in to help this struggling project, and interestingly enough, he did not know I was coming. When I was introduced to him and told him my purpose, he told me, "Well, I think we are just fine. The subs just need to follow the schedule I give them and we will all get along and finish the project." When I asked to meet with him, he refused. When he was asked to lead trade huddles as a part of a Lean system, he refused. To this day I am not actually sure what he wanted to do, but he definitely did not want to communicate. As I will share in more detail later on in this book, he was terminated for failure to perform in his role. After his departure another superintendent took over, began communicating with the trades and the team and got the project back on track even before I could return to help the project following my initial assessment. That is how crucial communication is. Even a failing project can turn around with consistent small doses of effective communication.

The plan should be communicated at a minimum of seven times for it to stick with the team.

Application and Challenge:

My challenge is to quadruple the amount of communication that we do on a daily basis. We really need to dig in here. The comment that we must repeat something seven times for it to stick is a minimum requirement. Until your team hears and understands it seven times, they have not even begun to rally behind the activity or the plan. It is a senior superintendent's job to repeat the plan in respectful and interesting ways so everyone can see as a group, know as a group, and act as a group. When you feel people are tired of hearing from you, please keep going. When you feel people are annoyed at you for repeating yourself, please keep going. When you feel people have had it with you explaining the plan in a caring and supportive way, you have only just begun. When you feel someone might punch you in the face because they are tired of hearing-congratulations, you are on the right track and off to a good start. The wisdom of a team is in figuring out how we are going to accomplish something. Where we are going and what we are doing is your job. And now I ask you—can your team figure out the how if they do not understand the where and the what? The answer is obvious. They need you. You are their...

Focus 5 - Team Captain

Introduction:

In the insightful book *The Captain Class: The Hidden Force That Creates the World's Greatest Teams*, author Sam Walker makes an interesting assertion that sports team dynasties were primarily held together by their team captains and not their star players. There was something different about these team captains that galvanized the team to win. Here are the seven most common traits of good team captains:

1. Extreme doggedness and focus in competition.
2. Aggressive play that tests the limits of the rules.
3. A willingness to do thankless jobs in the shadows.
4. A low-key, practical, and democratic communication style.
5. Motivates others with passionate nonverbal displays.
6. Strong convictions and the courage to stand apart.
7. Ironclad emotional control.

To be a great senior superintendent, you will need to develop these focuses in your style.

Story:

I worked with a project director who had a style like no other. He was focused, committed, and a great member of the team. His project teams knew he was in it to win. I remember one project where the schedule began to slip because of some design changes. The project team began complaining about the changes and slipped behind schedule allowing the project to get out of hand. The project director called me and we were able to recover. What I appreciated most was his team captain style versus boss style. He met all seven traits for being a good team captain. He would work diligently during the hard weeks and months of turning that project around. He did not just delegate this. He was aggressive in his determination to negotiate a good deal to the finish line with the owner. I remember him passionately discussing this with the owner's rep and getting a small extension to make the win possible.

He was willing to dive in and help with change orders and key roadblocks where he was needed and also willing to perform thankless jobs. He remained in control and always set an example. One day he brought in lunch for the project team and rewarded them for a job well done. But he didn't just want the job done; he wanted the team to be one. His style was superior in my mind because he leaned in with the team, led the team, and set the example for the team while he was serving the team. Only a few can accomplish this. And that project finished on time with a raving fan client, an intense finish, but a steady one that would not be classified as a crash landing. He won.

Bosses direct. Team captains set the example for and serve the team.

Application and Challenge:

I strongly recommend new senior superintendents reading Walker's *The Captain Class* to better understand what is expected from them as a leader. This book is wonderful when it comes to framing a proper mindset and paradigm of leadership. My challenge would be for every superintendent to assess whether they are barking orders or shaping a clear vision, setting an example, and tirelessly supporting the team while doing hard things alongside them. There is a big difference between telling and leading. Which type of leader are you? And what improvements could you make tomorrow to be the kind of leader you want to be? In order to rise to this challenge, you will need to learn how to be…

Focus 6 - Vulnerable

Introduction:

Great leaders who are senior superintendents are vulnerable. They are vulnerable by being open and confident enough with others to show up as an actual real human being. Great senior supers do not have to show up as the infallible captain of the ship. They need to show up as the captain—confident in the team with the trust of the team. They must allow themselves to be open to others even knowing they could be attacked.

Story:

The old style of leading among the superintendent ranks could be summed up by a bit of advice I was told by a general superintendent under whose leadership I grew up. He told me, "Jason, don't ever let them figure you out." His style was to keep people on their toes always guessing what kind of mood he was in. I think this gave him a sense of being in control. But his leadership was limited even though he was able to help build some large projects. He told me a story about a time when he kicked down the door of a project engineer's office when that PE wanted some time to cool down. He was having none of it. He railed on the PE in the staff meeting, followed her to her office after she shut the door, and then kicked it down. He got into quite a bit of trouble for that incident and it followed him throughout his career. She didn't have him figured out, and he did keep her on her toes, but it did not build a connection and it did not help the project. If he had leaned into vulnerability and communicated why his concern was important, he would have had a much different outcome. As it was, he continued to build the same size projects with the same size teams with the same amount of limited influence, while other general superintendents went on to improve entire business units and build billion dollar projects.

Always let them figure you out. Once they have you figured out, they can help care about the things you care about.

Application and Challenge:

There is something beautiful about a superintendent who can tell you how he or she is feeling about something instead of going on the attack. Ideally, a superintendent should be able to stand in front of a room of trade partners, share the plan, ask the questions, and receive the feedback while not getting defensive. If there is a disagreement, you can train your first thought to be, "Okay, what other options are there for us?" and, "Let me share how I am feeling and what I am concerned about" instead of becoming defensive. This takes practice for sure, but when you show up as vulnerable, you can gather the good will of the team to solve the problem, and actually, to solve your problem. For further information about vulnerability, I recommend any of Brene Brown's books. Team captains and humble, vulnerable people usually remain in the shadows, but in your position you must be well....

Focus 7 - Advertised

Introduction:

Great senior superintendents are seen, known, and well-advertised. The days of "I just don't like being in the limelight or out in public" are over for you. You must be seen, you must have influence, and people must recognize you as someone in a role they can count on and go to. You cannot be invisible. Senior superintendents help prevent and fight fires. If there was a fire next to you right now what would you do first? Run? Leave? Both are good strategies. If you did not do one of those two you would find a fire extinguisher. But, if it is hidden, what good will it do you? When teams need prevention or help, can they see where the tool is that can help? Do they know you? Do you have influence? Can they see you? Not being well-advertised for a senior superintendent is a cowardly excuse to protect yourself and think of your own selfish interests, not what is best for the team. It is time to stop this and start thinking of others. People need to see their fire extinguisher.

Story:

I knew a project superintendent in Southern California who was a great builder. He ran teams well, knew the business, and was well liked by the owners. He was the total package. In fact, he was so well liked by his teams, many would request to stay with him or refuse to work on another project without him. I was able to work with him multiple times. There came a time when he was up for being promoted to general superintendent and he was told no. The answer? People did not know him. He had been too reclusive on his projects and did not have influence with the people in his same business unit. He was furious. After a few years of practicing being out in public view, helping other teams, and being at company events, he was promoted. And he is one of the best general superintendents I have ever seen. But, he was not good enough to slide past being widely known and advertised.

To be a leader at a general level, you must have influence at a general level.

Application and Challenge:

If you are or are on your way to becoming a senior superintendent, you need to be involved with the wider company. People are counting on you to help shape policy, improve company conditions, and scale training. If there are departments that need elevation or general roles that need to be mentored, your position gets to do it. In order to carry that out you must be known on a more general level. This can be easily implemented as you attend more company events, provide company training, tour projects, mentor others, and share on any appropriate type of company media. You must be known to get where you want to be, and if you are already there you need to be known to stay there. Now that you have influence, you can be...

Focus 8 - A Chief Reminding Officer
Introduction:

A senior superintendent is the CRO (Chief Reminding Officer) of the business unit. When the team needs training, he or she provides that but most of the time, people need to be reminded, not taught. It is the senior super's job to constantly reinforce key components of the project plan and schedule or to remind the project team of those key components. A good rule of thumb is that the item has not been communicated effectively or people have not been reminded until they hear you say something seven times. This is your job as CRO. You must remind everyone on the project or projects where they are going, how they are going to get there, and in what manner they will do it. You are the CRO which means you are also the Chief Culture Builder and Chief Communication Scaler.

Story:

When I was a field operations director at a large general contractor, the company had improvement, survey, schedule, and self-perform departments, but they were not all heading in a single direction. I read Patrick Lencioni's book, *The Motive: Why So Many Leaders Abdicate Their Most Important Responsibilities* and immediately began scheduling weekly meetings with each department to align their vision and direction. After about six to eighteen weeks (depending on the department), I was able to get those departments humming along so well that they were the envy of the company. We had to get a superintendent and field engineer huddle bi-weekly to get them going at the same pace. We started to be so effective that the PMs and PEs started to complain about not getting enough training and attention in the company.

Senior supers are Chief Reminding Officers. They get to tell everyone at least seven times where the company and operations are going. Only then can they go together and to the same destination.

Application and Challenge:

As a senior superintendent, you must have touch points with every part of the business you oversee. This will include your project or projects. Everyone on your projects and within your influence should know where the company is headed, how their group, division, or department can support, and how they can accomplish the goals to those targets. You get to remind them of that and the processes, procedures, and best practices that will enable them to accomplish their goals. My rule of thumb was if I can get into a recurring meeting with that group, I can remind them and teach them continually. The battle is won when the meetings begin. In order for you to remind and train, you will have to be...

Focus 9 - Well-trained and Developed
Introduction:

A senior superintendent cannot fake the skills of the trade. He or she must be well-trained with all the tools and systems that will be used. We used to have world class builders in our industry. Why? Because they were trained like world class builders. Sometime after 2007 and 2008, companies stopped training people to the degree they used to. If I remember back to my day, I was training in all aspects of safety and specific scopes like scaffolding, cement masonry, cranes, hoisting methods, and construction logistics. I was trained to know Excel, Bluebeam, AutoCAD, Revit, Sketchup, Navisworks Manage, all Office products, and more. I was trained to know CPM scheduling, short interval scheduling, Last Planner®, Scrum, PERT, Adept, and others with their associated applications. People I grew up with could perform surveying tasks, test concrete, inspect rebar with the best of inspectors, and create lift drawings as pretty as the contract drawings themselves. This has become a lost art. You must understand that there are no easy buttons when it comes to being great. It comes from rigorous, intentional, and well-done training.

Story:

I used to receive a lot of training from the company I worked for, but one day I got the idea that I would ask to take an AGC CM-BIM course so I could get the certification. I was allowed to spend 3K for the training and then passed the test to get my credentials. I was hooked. I then took the DBIA certification training, the CM-Lean certification training, and then went on to Leancor, Tony Robbins, and Rapport Leadership International. My first year of training outside the company cost me 3K. The second cost me 5K. The third cost me 7K. The fourth cost me 15K. The fifth cost me 30K. The sixth cost me 50K. And this year I will spend 125K on training. I can honestly say I have increased my salary double what the training cost was for that year. You will be compensated and promoted in direct correlation to how much training you receive. Should you spend that much money on training? Maybe not, but you should not fear it. I would have no hesitation to tell someone to put it on a credit card and go into debt for it. Why? Because you will get it back tenfold if you take the training, implement it, and add more value to your employer.

You will be paid commensurate with your training. If you want to make more, add more value. If you want to add more value, attend remarkable trainings.

Application and Challenge:

The application here is simple. Find the best world-class trainings that will push you to your limit. Then find a way to pay for it. Then attend it. And finally, implement everything you learn on your project or projects at a rapid pace even in the face of adversity. No one wants your stale parroted information you heard from someone else. People want fresh, practical, and value-add ideas from the best information available and through a person who has personally implemented it. Sometimes you will not get where you want to get through trainings alone. You may need to focus on…

Focus 10 - Getting a Mentor

Introduction:

In addition to training, everyone needs a mentor. The key to success is to read about, study from, and be around the people who have achieved what you want to achieve. This will hold true for business, finances, spirituality, health, and life in general. Mentors elevate the mentee. There is quite a bit of pulling yourself up by your boot straps that you can do, but nothing will increase the speed of your progress like getting a mentor.

Story:

The best thing that ever happened to me was to have mentors. At the risk of leaving someone out, I will tell you who some of my mentors have been:

Scott Berg - Elevated me into a training role when I was a field engineer. Taught me how to be a builder.

L.G. Willden - Mentored me with religion, morality, and ethics.

Brad Nelson - Taught me how to be a superintendent and a master builder. Being with Brad really elevated my career and started me on an accelerated trajectory.

Djuro Rosic - Mentored me into becoming a general superintendent. Taught me how to think on a larger scale.

Derek Kirkland - Mentored me into becoming a whole human being and construction professional. Taught me how to build teams and mentor people.

Ryan Young - Mentored me as a PM and taught me project management. Ryan told me I would change the industry. I believed him, and here I am today.

Brian Melcher - Mentored me in business and encouraged me to step out on my own.

David Brown - Contacted me out of nowhere to coach me on how to run a consulting practice and give me encouragement.

There have been so many people who have taken me under their wing, but the people I listed have had a direct impact on me and my life. They are positive voices in a sea of negativity. You need your positive voices. You need people who can elevate you. And last, but most important. Kate, my partner and eternal companion has coached me every step of my life and career. I have always had a mentor.

To be who you want to be, you have to be near the people who are already there and have become that.

Application and Challenge:

Write down what you want to become. Find that person. Then, go find a way to be mentored by that person or at least be in close proximity with him or her. You must do this. You deserve this. Also, you may have this wrong. You may have seen others stay close to a great leader, get promoted, and say to yourself, "That person was just her favorite. He was just lucky." Wrong! He wasn't lucky; he was close. He became what she was through proximity, and you will too if you take the same course. It is not about favorites, politics, or luck. It is about proximity. As I said before, the main influence in life has been my wife and partner. You will have the same support and blessing as you focus on...

Focus 11 - Your Family
Introduction:
Every good senior superintendent is also a great senior superintendent at home and has the support of home. No success can compensate for a failure at home, and a failure at home will determine failure at work. To be fully effective at work, you must be effective at home. Your role, whether new or old, has within it enough time for you to dedicate focus, time, and attention to the well-being and maintenance of your family. Whether this is important to you is irrelevant. As a leader you are a role model, and you cannot afford to set a bad example for others on your project. Senior leaders go home on time, they take vacations, and they go to appointments. Remember, your job is to communicate, and one of the main things you will communicate effectively on your projects is that we work to support our lives and families; we do not have families to support work. Obviously there is a balance there, but it should tip in the direction of family. I will close this introduction by also saying that supers who have to work over fifty-five hours constantly to get their jobs done are not good superintendents. Only the good ones can get it done within a normal time frame.

Story:

I quit my first real construction job because I had an imbalance. That sounds dramatic, but I can at least say I did something about it. When I came back to work I had my head on straight, and never again let work affect my family past reasonable limits. In the many boot camps I have been a part of, and when witnessing literally thousands of people reflect on their career, I have never heard remorse for not spending enough time at work. In fact, to the contrary, I have heard story after story lamenting how superintendents ignored their families to the detriment of their health, relationships, and marriages. They all would have given it all up if they could have gone back to fix it. You can prevent this from happening to you if you will just learn to care for your family. No one will remember what buildings you built, but you will remember the time spent with family. Additionally, after the age of 45, most of your goals, moments, and memories will be with family. Ask yourself, "Who will be with me in the latter part of my life?"

No success at work can compensate for a failure in the home.

Application and Challenge:

Schedule date night, time with kids, and family time first in your week. Don't argue with me and tell me you are too busy. Are you a good super? Well then, good supers know how to care for their family and work. Don't give me your excuses. I want happy spouses, partners, kids, and animals at home every week. Ask every member of your family what quantitative and qualitative time they would love to see from you and schedule it. Schedule it first and be where you say you will be. If you do this, you will have no regrets and you will leave a legacy beyond your imagination. If you care for your family, you have cared for the first wedge in...

Focus 12 - The Wheel of Life

Introduction:

Imagine a large circle on a piece of paper. There are wedges on that paper that make the circle look like a piece of pizza or a wheel with spokes. Now imagine that each wedge represents a different aspect of your life. Perhaps one wedge is health and fitness, another is finances, and another is spirituality. What these are titled is not as important as your wheel having wedges that represent all aspects of your life. Certainly you will have work and family relationships there. Now imagine the center of your circle represents a zero, and the outer edge of the circle represents a ten. What if you drew a line in each wedge for the score you have in that aspect of your life. Would it be balanced? Would it be even? Or, would it be jagged and disproportionate? Which type of wheel will take you farther and faster in life? The jagged one or the balanced one? The answer is obvious, and what is also obvious is the fact that we must be whole in life to be effective in any of our individual wedges including the work wedge.

Story:

I was asked to help a superintendent who was failing on a project. The project was behind schedule, riddled with bad morale, and the owner was very unhappy. I sat down with him and another senior leader at lunch and asked him how his life was going. He reported less than favorable marks in almost all aspects of life. Church was not going well, his marriage was hanging by a thread, he had neglected his health, and the list of sad marks went on and on. I remember telling him he needed a few wins in his life. I told him people can usually endure two or possibly three unsuccessful aspects to their lives, but not more than that. He immediately set to fixing the things he could. He got marriage counseling and tried to be more active at his church. He called me about a year after our two coaching sessions and reported that his life and work were going much better. Today he is successful because he focused on his wheel of life.

You cannot be successful in one aspect of your life and unsuccessful in others. You win with balance and lose with imbalance.

Application and Challenge:

I recommend assessing the various aspects of your life. Scale each of the following on a scale from one to ten and then make a game plan for how you can even out every aspect of your life using these categories:

- Finances
- Family
- Work
- Spirituality
- Mental Health
- Physical Body and Health
- Emotions
- Time

As you give more attention to the neglected aspects of your life, you will see the others rise. Some things in your life are going better than you think. Grade your effort and focus on those efforts in addition to your fulfillment in those areas, but you will only be truly fulfilled as you begin...

Focus 13 - Managing Stress

Introduction:

Stress is an interesting thing. If you would ask a large group of people, you would most certainly be told by the majority that stress is bad for you. And that would not be an entirely accurate statement. Distress is unhealthy for you, but Eustress may actually become the opposite. You see, when you are encountered by a situation that could be considered "stressful," your body can deal with it in multiple ways. Most certainly, your body will release cortisol, a stress hormone, but under certain circumstances, your body will also release oxytocin, which can increase your capacity and human connection with others. So I like to separate out the various types of stress into a minimum of four categories:

1. Stress from trauma, fear, or abuse. This is harmful stress that creates disconnection from other human beings.

2. Stress to meet a challenge. This type of stress, if viewed in a positive mindset, can help you to grow and expand your capacity.

3. Stress when being forced to learn something. This type of stress, if viewed in a positive mindset, can actually help you to learn.

4. Stress when you are nurturing others and coming together in a crisis. This type of stress can actually help you to build human connection.

The last three can be good types of stress. The key is your outlook and how you handle stress. I guess it would be fair to say that it still needs to be managed, and that you can manage it in a way that it becomes a good type of stress. For more information, I recommend *The Upside of Stress: Why Stress Is Good for You, and How to Get Good at It* by Kelly McGonigal.

Story:

During a recent experience as a business leader, I let myself get stressed by flying and being away from home. On the flight I texted Kate that I could not do this anymore. I felt run down and locked into a situation where I was working too hard for too long. When Kate talked to me she helped me to see a new perspective. She said, "Where do you get to go on these trips?" I replied, "Beautiful places like Florida." She then asked, "Who do you get to work with on a weekly basis?" I replied, "Wonderful people who care about changing the industry." And this went on and on until I realized I was really blessed and it was my decision to do this. My feelings about the trip changed and I began to enjoy it. The types of stress that come from abuse and trauma are legitimately damaging, but for most of the rest of our experiences, a change of perspective can help quite a bit.

Everything that happens to you can become a tool. A tool for good or bad. A tool for growth or regression. A tool for stress or elevation.

Application and Challenge:

I thought hard about whether or not to include this section because I do not want to diminish the effects of stress or situations where people experience harmful types of stress. Eventually, I decided to include it because so much of the stress we experience is exaggerated and can be easily changed into a good form of stress that builds connection. My hope is that this small section in the book can help anyone who is feeling stressed to reframe their experience and enjoy more of their work. This will become clearer as you focus on being…

Focus 14 - Masculine Empowered Versus Wounded

Introduction:

There is a large difference between a leader who is wounded versus empowered. We have heard from the old guard that stoicism, harshness, yelling, not showing vulnerability, and not letting people get to know them were desired attributes of a superintendent. Actually, that is a perfect description of woundedness. Why would someone be stoic? Because he has been hurt and is emotionally closed off. Why would someone be harsh? Because he has been hurt and will hurt you before you hurt him. It is based on fear. Why would someone... Well, okay. I will stop. You get the point. Behind the rough and tough exterior of the old guard is woundedness. People in their empowered state are not overcome with fear to the point of shutting down. Empowered people don't mind being vulnerable because they are confident and not overcome with the fear of being hurt. We must normalize empowered behavior and attributes, not the wounded ones. Behind all the rough and tough exteriors are hurt and fearful people or why the need for the protective shell?

Story:

I have worked with some of the best builders this industry has ever seen. Many of them would advocate abusive behavior in the name of leading a project. I think this may be the main reason people demonize command and control nowadays because they would command people and control people in abusive ways. They did not do this out of strength. They did this out of fear and hurt as I said before. Whenever I experienced a leader who

1. Was controlling
2. Was aggressive

3. Withdrew emotionally
4. Avoided people
5. Was competitive
6. Was abusive
7. Was unstable
8. Criticized
9. Condemned
10. Complained
11. Controlled

I knew I was dealing with someone who was hurt.

Whenever I interacted with a person who:

1. Was deeply present
2. Didn't judge
3. Was supportive
4. Had discipline
5. Was focused
6. Was logical
7. Was confident
8. Acted honestly
9. Was self-accountable
10. Had integrity
11. Acted humbly
12. Was responsible, and,
13. Showed up in a vulnerable manner

I knew I was dealing with someone who was whole, confident, and strong.

Bad behavior comes from fear and hurt, not strength.

Application and Challenge:

The challenge for all of us is to nurture our divine nature, not our injured facade. I cannot tell you exactly how to go from being injured to the point that you show up in a positive way with others, but I can help you to realize when it is happening. When you see others or yourself acting in the manner I have described above, please know it is not strength, it is weakness. The key here is to not engage with this behavior in yourself or others. A confident and strong builder will lead in a confident and caring manner and never display the attributes of an old American West cowboy. He will be open, vulnerable, caring, considerate, and show up as him or herself. If you do this you will have influence with those you seek to lead. If you can nurture your divine nature, the last thing to consider is avoiding...

The Blocks to Leadership - (Don't Be Held Back)

The list above can be very helpful in guiding a senior level superintendent to higher levels of success when leading her or his team. There will be blocks that, if not broken and removed, will attempt to hold us back from showing up in a vulnerable and approachable way. These are called the blocks to leadership. I was taught this by Rapport Leadership International in their Leadership Breakthrough courses. I am very appreciative to them for providing these for us to consider. There may be one, two, or many of these that are holding you back from showing up how you want to as a leader. To break through them, the first step is acknowledgement. The second step is to break the pattern when they are holding you back. The third step is to reframe and redirect your behavior to not only break them, but to walk through that wall or block to further success. Please read the summary of each of these and determine how you will overcome these blocks. If you follow this pattern and still cannot break through, join us for our Super/PM Boot Camps and I know you will not only break through these, but also become the leader you want to be.

Block 1 - Wanting To Be Liked

When we want to be liked, we avoid saying the hard things, making the hard decisions, and doing anything that would make someone else question whether they like us. I once heard a saying that stated, "People who do not say what needs to be said for fear of offending someone else are only thinking of him or herself." This is a block to leadership because leaders must do what is right, not what is popular. When you break through the block of wanting to be liked, you can make the kinds of hard decisions that leaders make.

Block 2 - Being Close-minded

Close-minded leaders are not using the genius of the team. That means they are not making good decisions and not implementing with the team. If you are close-minded because of fear or arrogance, you will succeed or fail by yourself and with limited capacity. Leaders have influence, and you cannot have influence if you do not listen to people and only direct traffic. Your influence will be mild at best, and people will likely do what they want behind your back which will hurt the energy and performance of the team. But if you can focus on being more open-minded, you will be able to leverage and use the wisdom of others, win them over, and have the team's help in implementing your projects.

Block 3 - Playing Savior

Depending on what you believe, there was only one Savior, and you and I are not Him. We play savior when we try to save or shield someone from the natural consequences of their actions. This only hurts the individual because lessons learned from circumstance are not only needed, they are crucial to personal and professional development. We play savior with people when we keep them from consequences, when we reduce the performance goal because they cannot meet them, or when we do their work for them so they do not have to be held accountable. If you stop playing savior with your people, they will experience the same hard knocks that made you great. Do not deprive them of that. Do not play savior.

Blocks 4 and 5 - Fear of Risk and Being Indecisive

A senior superintendent cannot be held back by the fear of risk or indecision. I can remember many times when a decision needed to be made about a risky venture, and it was the PM and super's job to make it. I remember having a tough decision on a project where we could use one large tower crane or two smaller ones. I weighed the capacity, speed, and setup costs of both options. After the analysis I was sure the two smaller ones would be just right for our project. As much as I wanted the team or someone else to decide, the concrete contractor, other trades, our team, and the PM were looking to me to make a decision. Was it risky? Yes. Not from a safety standpoint, but from a production and schedule standpoint it was risky. These types of decisions will come up again and again in the career of a senior superintendent. Failing to make these will only hurt you and the project. If you do your research, consider all options, prioritize safety, and gather the wisdom of the team, it is your job to make a decision, and fear of risk will hold you back from doing that. Senior supers do not let a fear of risk hold them back from tough decisions.

Block 6 - Being Too Critical

If you are too critical, you will not enable people to be their best selves or do their best work. There is a lot more explaining, teaching, coaching, mentoring, and enabling needed when delegating to others than criticism. Criticism is destructive to energy, morale, and engagement. You are too critical when you do not show appreciation for the best efforts of others. You will break through this when you appreciate the best in others and move forward with an encouraging approach that will garner the best efforts of the team.

Block 7 - Low Expectations

Respect equals high expectations. If you respect someone, you will also expect the best for them and of them. A senior superintendent cannot have low expectations of anyone on their project. Cleanliness, safety, organization, logistics, and operations have to be perfect. Everyone on the project site should find it hard work to elevate to the expectations of the senior super on site. You have low expectations when you tolerate bad behavior and low standards. You can break through this block by always having high expectations and mentoring people to rise to the level of your expectations. Remember, the success of any project is determined by the worst behavior the leader is willing to tolerate. Additionally, people will normally rise to the level of expectations of others in a social group. People deserve our respect, and therefore, they deserve high expectations.

Block 8 - Desire for Control Versus Empowerment

A senior superintendent must have control of his or her project, but that control is for operational systems, not people. People need to be taught, encouraged, and enabled. When supers are too controlling about the schedule, the plan, meetings, or the actions of people, he or she is diminishing others and their potential. Controlling behavior reduces the wisdom of the team down to one, it wastes resources, and it bottlenecks information and efforts. You can break through that block when you learn to delegate, mentor, and trust your team with critical assignments. Great leaders are empowering, not controlling.

Blocks 9 and 10 - Low Self-esteem and Low Self-worth

Low self-esteem and low self-worth is something we should be empathetic and sensitive to in ourselves and others, but we must also realize it can hold us back. Higher self-confidence comes from self-acceptance and self-care, and with practice, a person can increase their self-esteem and worth. We have low self-esteem and low self-worth when we diminish ourselves and our abilities. We are held back because we lack the needed confidence to lead and influence others on our projects as a consequence. We break through this when we learn to appreciate our inherent self-worth and properly esteem our intentions and the accomplishments we have made. As you increase your self-esteem and self-worth, your confidence and passion will enable you to influence others—which is the essence of leadership.

Block 11 - Focus on Problems, Not Opportunities

Projects are completed on time when project teams and leaders aggressively take advantage of opportunities to win and drive forward. Success does not come from being stagnant and in a defensive position. Just like in war, we must be constantly advancing. Gaining this ground is reserved for the opportunists, not the pessimists. There is a very important point I want to make. When it comes to being realistic about where we are, we need to be realists. Wishful thinking or seeing through rose colored glasses never helped anyone or any organization. I am talking about considering what we can do in the future. The present belongs to the realists, and the future belongs to the opportunists and optimists. To be a great leader you must have a mixture of both a focus on problems and opportunities. Leaning too much toward the problems will diminish your range of view and your effectiveness in moving your project and company forward.

Block 12 - Having a Lack of Purpose

This is a big one... Let me ask you a question. Why is it important to run a good job? Why is it important to make money? Why is it important to get home on time? Why is it important to take care of your health? Why is it important to serve? If you do not know these answers you do not fully know your purpose and your why. And why would that be a problem? Because without purpose there is no excellence. Without purpose there is no motivation to be better and do better. If I had a nickel for every time a crusty superintendent told me, "Why would I change? I have always brought projects in on time," I would at least be able to afford a fancy dinner at a five star restaurant. These supers don't know why they would change because they lack motivation. They lack motivation because they lack purpose. It would be obvious why we should run better projects if that super understood the purpose of respecting people, serving, building families, improving the industry, taking care of the customer, etc. But without a purpose like the examples I just gave you, it is just another job, just another paycheck, and just another day. You can break through this block when you look past material things, stop being mediocre, and live a life of purpose.

Blocks 13 and 14 - Fear of Embarrassment and Rejection

Fear of embarrassment is akin to wanting to be liked. A person who does not want to be embarrassed or rejected craves the attention, approbation, and acceptance of others. Ultimately it is a selfish venture. We are held back by this block when we fail to do the right thing just because we might be embarrassed. We are held back when we fail to do the right thing because we fear being rejected by someone we care about or admire. We can break through this block when we value doing the right thing and making the right decisions over our own selfish desire to look good and be accepted by people.

Blocks 15 and 16 - Having to Be Perfect and Having to Work Hard to Be Loved

Which of us did not learn to work hard and make a decent living because of a feeling we needed to be perfect and work hard? For most of us, we learned that to be loved by our family, we had to excel and work harder than anyone else. This was a great start, but now it could be keeping you from what you need to be doing. You see, in a senior superintendent role, you are "doing" hardly anything. You are explaining, teaching, mentoring, and enabling your team to do the "doing." If you are too wrapped up in wanting to be perfect, do everything perfectly, and work hard, you will find yourself doing things you don't belong doing, and being places you don't belong being. It is your job to lead, and sometimes that does not look like hard work or perfection. To break through these blocks, you must prioritize doing your role well, stop the busyness, appearing to work hard, and being perceived as perfect in what you do.

Breaking Through

As we have written above, breaking through these blocks to leadership is absolutely crucial. Although they are normal and common for most people, you cannot be fully effective and hide behind these fears and insecurities too long. You must find a way to intentionally break through if you are going to be great. As of this writing, the best method for doing this is to attend an immersive leadership course designed to elevate your performance and help you manage your fears. Elevate Construction offers boot camps for this very purpose. There are many other organizations that offer this type of training as well. The two I am most familiar with are Tony Robbins' *Unleash the Power Within* and *Leadership Breakthrough 1* by Rapport Leadership International. Whatever you choose to do, you deserve to break through to higher performance.

The 7 Deadly Sins - (Don't Let Unlearned Skills Slow You Down)

There are seven deadly sins that will either hold back a superintendent or hinder him if accidentally promoted. These show up with most superintendents who get stuck early in their career. It is interesting to note that studies show superintendents get stuck right around the Super 2 level as shown at the end of this book. We have also tracked why this happens, and have come up with the seven deadly sins of being a superintendent. Also interesting is the correlation with being a field engineer. All of these sins can be prevented by learning the fundamentals of field engineering. It would naturally stand to reason that we focus on field engineer training at Elevate Construction as a main focus. But if you were not a field engineer, and if you cannot go through that experience, we can at least mention these for you here to help your career. Beware of these sins because they will hold you back and hurt your career.

Sin #1 - Not Holding People Accountable

Sin #1 is not holding people accountable. This is one of the greatest sins because a superintendent that cannot hold people accountable in a professional manner, and one who does not have control of his project is ineffective to the point of uselessness (as I stated in my previous book). There are four types of construction managers: leaders, managers, accountants, and victims. In short, a leader will anticipate problems in the future and prevent them. A manager will see problems and react to them to fix them. An accountant monitors problems and tracks them. A victim neither knows what is wrong or has the ability to fix it. The bottom two descriptions, victims and accountants, don't really serve any real purpose for a construction company. They are worthless. The leader is obviously the ideal, and at least the manager reacts, but in both situations they are holding people accountable. So, you see, the ability to hold people accountable is the difference between being a leader or manager or an accountant or victim. The bottom line is that a senior leader must be able to hold people accountable.

Leading the project requires holding people accountable and leading other supers also requires it. The senior part of senior superintendent presupposes the ability to lead others and hold them accountable. If a super will not learn this or has not, he should not be promoted to higher levels of leadership, and they often aren't. They will get stuck in assistant or helper roles where they do things instead of lead people. I remember a senior superintendent in title only who wanted and received the title when he hired on, but who was not qualified for the role. He knew how to build, was decent at scheduling, but he would not lead huddles, mentor other supers, or really communicate in any real way. He did not have control of the project and was not enforcing safety, cleanliness, or organization rules and guidelines. This became such a problem that the project executive met with him and the PM to resolve the issue. During the meeting he admitted he was incapable of filling the role of a senior superintendent and asked for the title of construction manager or schedule manager instead. His idea was that he could fill out the schedule and manage it daily while the assistants did the real work of communicating and collaborating with the trades. He was fired. You cannot abdicate the responsibility of leading and holding others accountable.

Sin #2 - Not Delegating

Delegation is the key to entering higher levels of leadership. First let me be clear about what I mean. Certain tasks must be delegated and they must be delegated effectively. As stated before, a senior super should do what only he or she can do and only what he or she should do. All other important and non-urgent items should be delegated. To delegate, you must remember to select the person, discuss with them the task, clearly define expectations, and give them time to execute the task. Then you check in with them periodically and help them accomplish the task if necessary. Appropriately and professionally holding them accountable to expectations and the deadline is important here as I said in Sin #1. This is delegation. The sin is when leaders fail to delegate. Why is this a sin? For two reasons. If the leader or would-be leader is to fulfill a senior role, he or she must be steering the ship or the fleet and be focused on being a good captain. This cannot be done if the would-be leader is down below doing lower level chores that he or she was unable to delegate. Secondly, the primary reason for a senior level leader is to mentor others. How can someone mentor others if they are not given the chance to perform tasks and learn? The answers are simple here.

I knew a project manager who would not delegate anything. His answer was always, "I will do that" or "I will get back to you." He never, and I literally mean never, trusted anyone on the team to make decisions or to carry out tasks. I never did find out why, but I assume he wanted the credit, loved being needed, and could not find that balance between delegating and checking in at the right time. I do know he was a perfectionist and did not trust others to do it as well as he did. He called me one time to help him recover his project. He was really struggling and about to get in trouble for not delivering it on time. I think that is ironic because it took him three months to schedule the visit with me because he would not trust me or anyone else to coordinate it. Once I was able to visit the project and gave him a recovery plan, he didn't even schedule the first meeting because he was "really backed up." He was demoted and assigned to manage change orders after that. You cannot fail to delegate if you want to be in a senior role or develop others.

Sin #3 - Having the Plan in His or Her Head

This third sin is a hateful and deplorable one. I can't stand it when supers have the plan in their head. All the trades run around confused because they have to ask the super every question. It looks like hours of wasted time every single day. It is disgusting. Most of the time the super keeps things in his head simply to feel important or to feel in control. Both reasons are maddening. The feeling of empowerment at having to answer all the questions and be sole savior of the project gives this type of super such a feeling of importance and rush of adrenaline that almost becomes an addiction. I hope you are feeling my disdain for this habit, and I pray you find a similar hatred for this behavior. When would-be leaders do this, they waste the time and money of trade partners, create chaos, and lose the project an incalculable amount of time. It is disrespectful, unprofessional, selfish, and again, disgusting. I don't want to hear the excuse of not being able to make a schedule or draw visuals or not being good with computers. First of all, if you are under forty-five years old, the only excuse for not being able to use a computer and make a schedule or visual is laziness and indolence. For everyone else, I suggest getting a large piece of paper and pencils.

I remember a superintendent that would not get the plan out of his head. He was constantly stressed and running around trying to figure out what was going on. During my visit I saw him running from place to place seemingly looking for something to calm him. I remember thinking the thing that would calm him was a piece of paper, a pen, and a good coordination meeting with the foreman. He constantly told me he just did not know how to get the plan out of his head. I realized something then and there. Most of these people actually don't have a plan. They are just saying they do. So when you hear someone say the plan is in their head, that might mean they don't have a plan at all. After a few days of helping him we were able to make a schedule for the project. The team loved it and bought into it right away. He still felt uncomfortable after we made the plan and stabilized the project. I was not sure why, but I can report that the assistant super ran with the plan and schedule and the systems used to continually refine it with the trades. The super in this story was removed from the project and later told me he did not think he belonged in construction at all. I have seen this over and over. Whether the person has a plan or does not have a plan, it must be fixed. Either get it out of your head and on paper, or make one with your team. A superintendent without a visual plan is like a racehorse without legs.

Sin #4 - Little or No Builder Experience

We have supers getting promoted right out of college without having spent time in the field as engineers, foremen, or assistants working with crews. This is a problem because they are not learning key skills. Every up and coming superintendent should be able to do the following:

1. Translate a 2D set of plans to a 3D image in their mind.
2. Piece together details from multiple sources.
3. Understand how building components come together.
4. Be able to visualize elevations and a coordinate system.
5. Visualize and piece things together to build.

There are so many builders who do not know how to do this. Why? Again, because they were never field engineers, foremen, or assistants helping crews in the field. Here is my question...if you have never made a lift drawing from multiple sources, do you really know how to read drawings? If you have never run a traverse, performed survey and layout tasks, and shot elevations, do you really know how to visualize things spatially? If you have never had to create a model in Revit or another application, can you really translate drawings into a 3D image in your mind? I could go on, but there is no need. The answer is obvious. People nowadays think that the role of a superintendent is about pointing and directing. They are wrong. It is about knowing how to build, understanding the fundamentals, and being able to keep up with your trades in a coordination meeting. It is not about bossing people around and making random decisions.

I knew a superintendent who was hired as a senior level superintendent. He seemed like a nice guy, but he was not a builder. I remember asking him a question about the drawings. He looked through a few, shrugged his shoulders, and then asked his field engineer to find out. He stood up and said, "I've got to go on a field walk." He did not have builder experience and he did not know what he was doing. I found out two weeks later that the trades did not like him because he would revert to yelling and bossing people around on the floors. A few of the foremen asked for him to be removed because he was unrealistically barking orders and never helping them. He was fired. You cannot just run around and bark orders with your authority. We need real builders that will lean in and support our trades and last planners. If we have people that do not know how to build, they would perhaps be better big box store security guards. At least there they could boss people around and not know what they are doing and get away with it.

Sin #5 - A Lack of Organization

A superintendent who is not organized is an interesting thought. Superintendents get paid to organize and bring order to projects. Why would we hire one who couldn't organize their room, office, phone, or truck? How someone does the small things is how they do the big things. If a super cannot even keep their voice message inbox clean and organized, how in the world would they organize millions of dollars, millions of components, and hundreds of people? Sometimes I feel like this is so simple, but we make it so hard. You hire the results you want on-site. If you want an organized project, you hire an organized person. If you want a punctual project, you should hire a punctual person. Let me tell you something that will always be true. It is impossible to hire someone who is unorganized and expect him to organize a project. You can judge this by his appearance, how he keeps his truck, his office, his phone, his hair, and his desk.

I can recall a superintendent who ran a horribly unorganized and dirty project. I still don't know why we thought he could do it, but we gave him a chance anyway. I walked into his job trailer one day and his trash can was full, his desk had wrappers on it like the computer programmer in Jurassic Park, he had forgotten his belt, and there were holes in his pants. This guy was a mess. The walls were barren in the trailer and the signs he ordered were collecting dust out back. Even his truck was a reflection of the way he regarded his work. Every crevice was packed with something. There were coffee cups everywhere, coffee stains, and banana peel on the dash. I could go on, but I get annoyed just thinking about him. Needless to say, his project was also a shambles. I made the recommendation he be let go, and the client I was working with fired him. After his departure, the team he'd been working with started to excel. If you are not organized, you cannot organize a construction project, and you will thankfully get stuck.

Sidenote: You may think I'm mean for happily reporting that these people were fired. I do not default to firing people. I believe in coach, coach, coach, coach, and then fire. In every example I have given, the person had plenty of time to accept coaching, mentoring, and more coaching. Their termination was a decision. Additionally, I am sure there are places where they can work and use their skills. The point is they cannot be superintendents. They chose to not be qualified.

Sin #6 - Not Using Technology

A superintendent who does not know how to use technology is like a backhoe operator who does not know how to run equipment. I will repeat what I said before. If you are under forty-five-years old there is no excuse for not using computers and technology. Most of us grew up with computers for crying-out-loud! For those between the ages of forty-five and sixty-five, I will say you are still young and can still learn. For those above sixty-five years old, I would say you are still young and can still do it. Really, there is no excuse for this. Not knowing how to use a computer, phone, or technology is now analogous to saying, "I don't know how to read" or, "I don't know addition and multiplication." It is absurd. And lest you think I am being dramatic and negative here, I will remind you that my job is to move you forward. You should not be technology illiterate, and anyone who has sympathy for you if you are doesn't really care about you or the people you lead. This knowledge is critical. You should know how to fully use your phone, the applications on your phone, your messages, Microsoft Word, Outlook, Excel, and Bluebeam at a minimum.

I remember a superintendent who said he could not use computers and chose not to. He was accidentally promoted to a senior superintendent level position and was asked to run large projects. He found a way to finish them, but he did it at the expense of all the trade partners. He attempted to get the plan out of his head alright, but he did it through a scheduler who had to shadow him daily on the project. I helped him to start pull planning sequences and creating look-aheads and weekly work plans. He bought in for a while, but there were too many days when his scheduling assistant was not on-site so he reverted to telling people what to do and changing plan all the time. It was chaos. As we monitored his project, it continued to lose money, be dirty, chaotic, and unorganized. He could not stand the accountability, did not appreciate where the company was going, and quit. Last year I heard he was blissfully making another company's life a nightmare by overextending and exhausting the trade partners over there. What a disaster. He could not run the tech so he reverted to stupid and dangerous techniques for running the field. There is no excuse for a superintendent who cannot use the tools of the trade. That means computers and technology.

Sin #7 - Not Learning Continually

When I say not learning I mean this person learned something then became stagnant. Did that job and now does it the same way thirty years later. Did that formwork and now does it twenty-five years later. Learned that one concept and has stuck to it for decades with moderate success. I am talking about a fixed and stagnant mindset. I hear of supers who have not read a book since high school, leaders who have never been through training since orientation, who have never had a coach or mentor. This is not only irresponsible, it is dangerous. Could you imagine a doctor who has not read a book or medical journal since college? Could you imagine a pilot who has not had training since their orientation? Could you imagine a military unit without mentors and coaches? Dangerous right? What makes the role of a super different? Supers lead hundreds of people with millions of dollars at stake at an incalculable risk. They must be trained. We have to stop allowing them to lead and not be trained. Humans do not naturally progress and get more enlightened. They retrograde, degenerate, become more perverse, and get stuck if they do not have additional light and knowledge from learning.

A superintendent was hired by a company to lead a one hundred and forty million dollar project. I asked him some questions about his background and in the process of trying to connect I got the "I haven't read a book since high school," answers just like I have in the past. It was funny (or not funny) to hear members of my team report two weeks later that he started to lecture the management team on the project about holding people accountable. He said, "I agree with Elevate that we need to hold people accountable. There was a concrete contractor that wasn't doing what I wanted so I walked through their newly placed concrete to teach them a lesson." I almost lost my mind when I heard, and the team went on to explain they pushed back on this idea and suggested a better approach. You will be happy to know that this particular supervisor continued to argue his point of view for about thirty minutes until the team got tired of talking about it. He was fired. You cannot be ignorant and neglect to stay current with trainings, books, events, and mentoring. Think about it. Do you want someone leading your job with the same knowledge they had in high school? Absolutely not. If you don't want to walk through your trades' newly placed concrete like a complete a-hole, I suggest you pick up the learning and reading habit. People who do not read and learn constantly should not be superintendents.

Field Position Levels

Below we have listed the general role from Super Level 6 to Super Level 1. The purpose is to entice you to higher levels of achievement, and provide a guide for you to evaluate your progress. Some companies have modified versions of this field progression list, so make sure you are aligned with your specific company.

A. Field Operations Director - SUPER 6 – Operational Excellence, Balanced Teams, Reduce Risk, Allocate Resources

    i. Role:

        1. Ensures projects are safe, clean, organized, with high morale

        2. Develop/Direct

            a. People

            b. Processes

            c. Resources

            d. Teams

            e. Operations implementation in field

        3. Responsible for several General and Project Superintendents, General Foreman, Laborers/Craft. Responsible for field operations, allocation of staff, work processes, interface with

scheduling, preconstruction, survey, BIM, and other departments
4. Roadblock remover for resources
5. Improves all aspects of field operations within business
6. Helps struggling projects and project teams
7. Runs Superintendent meetings
8. Meets with Directors
9. Executive level management
10. Communicates company's goals and vision
11. Supports development and implementation of operations initiatives
12. BD support in project pursuits for
    a. Logistics
    b. Phasing
    c. Schedule

ii. Skills:
1. Capable of managing large, complex and multiple projects over $250 million. 20+ years' experience
2. Executive level skills
3. Advanced problem-solving skills
4. Lean champions
5. Field Engineer champions
6. Construction methodologies champions
7. Communicates well with Project Directors
8. IPD champions
9. + SUPER 5 skills

iii. Emotional Intelligence:
    1. Advanced team building skills
    2. Proficient with training
    3. Master culture builders

iv. Outcomes:
    1. Projects are safe with a presence in field
    2. Projects are clean and organized
    3. All departments continue to support projects more effectively
    4. Teams are built that work well together
    5. All Superintendents are being trained well
    6. The role of General Superintendent is functioning well

B. General Superintendent – SUPER 5 – Build Teams, Oversee Projects from Start to Finish, Predictable Results [Leader]

i. Role:
    1. Ensures projects are safe, clean, organized, with high morale
    2. Oversees multiple projects
    3. Solves problems with staff, manpower, and materials
    4. Roadblock remover for projects
    5. Manages allocation of Craft
    6. Responsible over several Project Superintendents, General Foreman, Laborers/Craft. Responsible for operational stability of projects.

7. Performs monthly and quarterly risk audits
8. Assists in Superintendent and Field Engineer training
9. Develops Craft to enter salary positions or Lead, Foremen, General Foreman positions
10. Oversees field operations from preconstruction to closeout
11. Supports and improves self-perform work
12. Develops trade partner relations
13. Is current with best industry practices
14. High team building focus
15. Oversees process from start to finish on project – the constancy with the Project Director /Project Executive
16. Leads in emerging industry practices

ii. Skills:
1. Capable of managing large complex and multiple projects over $160 Million. 18+ years' experience
2. Understands all aspects of construction in the field
3. Proficient in proposals and with sales relationships
4. Project startup champions
5. + SUPER 4 skills

iii. Emotional Intelligence:
1. Team building
2. Knowledge of IPD
3. Approachable
4. Excellent communicator

iv. Outcomes:
1. Projects are safe with a presence in field
2. Projects are clean and organized
3. On-site superintendents are mentored and feel supported
4. Project transfer from preconstruction to construction is smooth
5. Every project has an effective plan to succeed
6. Every project finishes on time without a crash landing
7. Every project has check-ins that allow resources to prevent problems
8. Craft is developed and every project has competent site control

C. **Senior Superintendent – SUPER 4 – Master Planner and Organizer, Sees the Future, Large Scale [Emerging Leader]**
   i. Role:
   1. Ensures projects are safe, clean, organized, with high morale
   2. Ensures all field systems are being used properly
   3. Plans and coordinates large or complex projects
   4. Roadblock remover for project
   5. Manages and allocates manpower
   6. Manages and allocates materials
   7. Master planner and scheduler
   8. Owner interface champion

9. Trains Supers and Field Engineers
10. Develops Craft into salaried positions
11. Responsible over several lower level Superintendents, General Foreman, Laborers/Craft
12. Responsible for steering the ship

ii. Skills:
1. Capable of managing complex and/or multiple projects over $100 Million. Minimum 15 Years' Experience
2. Increased complexity of projects and systems
3. Can oversee all phases of preconstruction
4. Can oversee commissioning
5. Milestone alignment champion
6. Complete understanding of all scheduling systems
7. Can interface with all project management systems and software
8. Can oversee entire project team
9. Learning and developing preconstruction and proposal support
10. Able to completely control project for operational excellence
11. + SUPER 3 skills

iii. Emotional Intelligence:
1. Able to provide clarity for multiple areas of the project
2. Manages people, goals and performance

3. Advanced understanding of Lean – has read *The Goal*
4. Team building strategies
5. Familiar with the *33 Strategies of War* and *The Art of War*

   iv. Outcomes:
1. Project is safe with a presence in field
2. Complete project control with operational excellence
3. High performing team
4. Project is clean and organized
5. Project is aligned
6. No lasting issues with manpower or procurement
7. All geographical areas of project are aligned
8. Every group is working effectively
9. On-site supers are mentored and supported

D. Project Superintendent – SUPER 3 – Plan and Organize a Project [Executing Well]

   i. Role:
1. Ensures project is safe, clean, organized, with high morale
2. High engagement in safety management
3. Plans and schedules work – holds milestones
4. Plans manpower and materials for project
5. Removes roadblocks
6. Oversees other Superintendents

7. Manages risk for project
8. Project setup and overall management
9. Manages materials
10. Owner interface champion
11. Responsible for Superintendents and Assistant Superintendents, General Foreman, Laborers/Craft. Responsible for organization, work methods, scheduling, cost control, conformity with drawings and specs, workmanship (QC) either directly or through a General Foreman or Foreman
12. Oversees Carpenters and other resources on project
13. Oversees Field Engineers
14. Ensures team is healthy

ii. Skills:

1. $50-100 Million dollar projects. 10 to 15 years' experience
2. Creates and manages a Schedule in P6
3. Operates all scheduling systems
4. Plans and manages complex logistics
5. Advanced communication skills verbally and in writing
6. Uses all PM computer systems and tech on-site
7. Strong with MEP
8. Procures and sets up cranes, shoring, and other complex construction means and methods
9. Oversees punch list and closeout

10. Oversees inspection systems, final inspections, and testing
11. Weekly schedule updates
12. Leads project Operations Meetings
13. Understands key Field Engineering principles
14. Understands how to use BIM
15. Negotiates with AHJs
16. Proficient with permitting and compliance
17. + SUPER 2 skills

iii. Emotional Intelligence:
1. Effective Team Leader – has read *The Advantage*
2. Solid understanding of Lean principles – has read *The Toyota Way*
3. Able to provide clarity for the project and communicate plan and strategy – has read *The Four Obsessions of an Extraordinary Executive*
4. Advanced communication and leadership skills and setup

iv. Outcomes:
1. Project is safe with a presence in field
2. Project is clean and organized
3. Project is on schedule
4. Everyone always knows the plan and their commitments to reach it
5. Milestones are always aligned
6. Team is functioning well
7. Trade Partners and self-perform are effective and there is high morale

a. **Superintendent – SUPER 2 – Plan and Execute Work**
   i. Role:
      1. Ensures project is safe, clean, organized, with high morale
      2. Short-interval planning champion
      3. Executes work
      4. Milestone alignment with project schedule
      5. Proactively engages in safety
      6. Responsible over lower level Superintendents, General Foreman, Laborers/Craft. Responsible for organization, work methods, scheduling, and conformity with drawings and specs, workmanship (QC) either directly or through a General Foreman or Foreman
      7. Responsible for production
   ii. Skills:
      1. $15-49 Million dollar projects. 5 to 10 Years' Experience
      2. Can create a vision and strategize
      3. Oversees short-interval planning
      4. Can run meetings and phase planning meetings
      5. Oversees weekly work planning
      6. Oversees day work planning
      7. Can run daily Foremen Huddles and Morning Worker Huddles
      8. Can supervise self-perform work
      9. Can mentor Field Engineer program
      10. Uses procurement log as a tool for alignment with project schedule

11. Can develop phase/sequence plans and CPM schedules
12. Impact control planning, ICRA, ISLM, and MOP management
13. + SUPER 1 skills

iii. Emotional Intelligence:
1. Understands how to implement change – has read *Switch*
2. Fits the ideal team player
3. Can oversee and interface with Owner, Trades, Team, and Public
4. Basic understanding of Lean principles – has read *2 Second Lean*
5. Interacts well with Owner

iv. Outcomes:
1. Project is safe with a presence in field
2. Project is clean and organized
3. All planning systems work onsite
4. There is always a plan for the next 6 weeks

b. **Assistant Superintendent – SUPER 1 – Safety and Quality Presence in the Field, Executes Work [a learning Super]**
   i. Role:
   1. Ensures area is safe, clean, organized, with high morale
   2. Supervises self-perform crews
   3. Onsite logistics control – cleanliness and organization

4. Safety supervision – safety presence in field
   5. Works with onsite crews for quality implementation
ii. Skills:
   1. $5 -15 Million dollar projects. 3 to 5 Years' Experience
   2. Computer skills for email, Excel, and personal organization
   3. Engages, resolves, and closes issues
   4. Able to generate flow on a project
   5. Is a quality champion
   6. Can create a 3 week look ahead plan and implement on the project
   7. Learning
      a. BIM
      b. Planning for safety
      c. Learning about job costs
iii. Emotional Intelligence:
   1. Able to work with Trade Partners
   2. Integral with project team
   3. Ability to mentor
iv. Outcomes:
   1. Project is safe with a presence in the field
   2. Project is clean and organized
   3. Deliveries are scheduled and organized
   4. Owner feels we are delivering quality
   5. Self-perform is successful

Senior Superintendent Commandments

There are certain principles and actions that every role must carry out to effectively succeed. These are summarized and listed below as the Senior Superintendent Commandments. Following these Commandments will ensure that you will be successful as a superintendent.

1. Start your day by prioritizing your task list. If you don't have a task list, create one.
2. Start out every interaction, visit, or engagement with a deep look into safety. People should know that will be the first thing you will dig into.
3. Ensure other supers are studying the drawings for thirty minutes every day.
4. Ensure all scheduling systems are working properly.
    a. Master schedule
    b. Short-interval planning
    c. Day planning
    d. The huddle system
    e. Visual communication of the schedule
    f. Reporting
5. Take a reflection walk with a member of the team when on-site and ensure he or she is taking notes and sending out assignments.

6. Always ensure the project team has the resources to do their jobs well.
7. Always know the financial status of the project.
8. Always remove roadblocks as one of your top priorities to clear the path for the team.
9. Ensure management of the supply chain and procurement systems are working perfectly.
10. Manage, coach, and mentor the team. Do not leave the project without elevating a team member.
11. Do your job:
    a. Build the team
    b. Have the difficult conversations
    c. Manage, coach, and mentor
    d. Ensure the team has remarkable meetings
    e. Scale clarity throughout the project and align the team

Senior Superintendent Daily, Weekly, and Monthly Tasks

Every senior superintendent must do certain things daily to be successful. Below is a list of items you can measure daily to ensure you are winning.

Daily Checklist Items:
1. Scale communication to teams
2. Receive scaled roadblocks from teams
3. Prompt communication with Owner about change conditions
4. Ask the right questions about safety that morning
5. Remove roadblocks for the team fanatically
6. Study the drawings

Weekly Checklist Items:
1. Check on team health
2. Review roadblock tracking systems
3. Safety check in
4. Review exposures
5. Review job costs
6. Review key submittals
7. Check on procurement process

8. Meaningful mentoring of supers and FEs
9. Participate actively in the project schedule update (also study schedule alone once a week)
10. Check in with owner in person or by phone
11. Quality Observations and FOWs needed
12. Dive into 3 things while on the project
13. Check cleanliness and organization of the site

Check Monthly:
1. Project risk assessment review
2. Meaningful check in with the supers (Overall Team Management)
3. Project KPI check in
4. Walk the project
5. BIM check in
6. Check in on pay apps
7. Review training for team
8. Do something for one of your owners when we don't expect anything from them
9. Dive into 3 things
10. Review schedule health
11. Check markups and totals for Job Cost Reporting
12. Check on Change Order organization

Overall Check ins:
1. Safety
2. Quality
3. Schedule

4. BIM
5. Cost/Financials
6. Procurement
7. Self-Perform
8. Risks
9. Buyout
10. RFIs
11. Submittals
12. Change Orders
13. Site Utilization
14. Pay Applications
15. Team Health

THE ART OF THE BUILDER

Project Audit

You can use this checklist to help you implement the concepts from this book. Do you have these items implemented? If not, what is your plan?

Schedule:
- Team has a significant performance challenge to focus on.
- Team has a milestone or milestones they are aggressively working toward.
- Master schedule is used as a tool for triggering work and procurement and is updated weekly.
- Make-ready scheduling is done 120 days out and used for ordering manpower and materials.
- Weekly Work Plan is created weekly in Trade Partner Weekly Tacticals.
- Day Plans are created in the Daily Foreman Huddle.
- Communication is getting to the Workers in the Daily Worker Huddle.
- Day Plan is posted in one location for the entire project.
- Superintendent is in weekly procurement meetings.

Operations:
- Team has fanatical roadblock removal systems.
- Team Weekly Tactical is effective and held on time.

- Team Daily Huddle is held and effective.
- Trade Partners grade the GC weekly.
- Craft has:
    - Remarkable Bathrooms.
    - Remarkable Lunch Area.
- Team coverage is discussed daily and planned weekly.
- Quality process is managed in team meetings.

Safety:
- Safety training is being rolled out in an effective manner.
- Weekly safety walks are done weekly.
- Daily Worker Huddles are held daily.
- Team has zero tolerance implemented.
- Safety permits are issued and reviewed daily.
- PTPs reviewed daily by geographical area.
- Project is perfectly clean.
- Project is perfectly organized.
- Project has a daily system to correct safety, logistics, and cleanup items.

Super Duties:
- Daily reports
- Observations
- Progress photos weekly

Project Expectations:
- Everyone knows how to **be safe** in their task.
- Everyone knows **what they are installing.**

- Everyone makes **improvements daily.**
- Keep **bathrooms clean.**
- Be **good neighbors** and take care of the customers' needs.
- Nothing **hits the floor.** No materials, trash, or other items hit the floor.
- **Just-In-Time** deliveries and scheduled deliveries - Create correctly sized inventory buffers for all materials and coordinate daily.
- All **cords off the floor** and managed in a remarkable way.
- Everything **on wheels**, Greenies, or painted pallets.
- All **accessways are clear** at all times.
- Organized workspaces - **Everything should be clean and organized.** There is a place for everything, and everything in its place.
- **Pull work** behind you. Nothing gets left behind; clear and sweep your areas, and leave a complete area.

The Measurement of a Great Project

Some people think the measurement of a good project is to be on budget and on schedule. I think this is a myopic view. I think the measure of success is much higher, and you either make the grade, or you do not. There are no points for somewhere in between. Here is the full measure of a great project:

1. The project was safe with a remarkable culture.
2. The project was built with high quality.
3. The project was within ten percent of the original profit targets.
4. Trade partners were successful in general.

5. The team was high functioning and happy.
6. People on the team met their career goals while there.
7. The owners and designers are raving fans.

The measurement of a great project is one of the most important considerations of your leadership. You must elevate your standards if you want to be great. The measurement of a great project cannot be defined only by finishing on time. Most projects in our industry do not finish on time, and the ones that do, finish at a considerable expense to the lives of the workers, the safety of the people on the project, their families at home, and the resources and the finances of our trade partners. This is not acceptable, and it is not the measure of success. A project is only successful when it is wonderfully safe, when it is built with quality from every aspect of the work, when production is managed and maintained throughout so that trade partners can make money when the team is balanced and feels happy to work on-site. It should feel like they're at Disneyland enjoying the ride from start to finish, even though the scary and hard times. It is successful when the owner is a raving fan, and when everything that we do on the construction project holds respect for people, our neighbors, and the customer's end goal. Additionally, we can't exploit the people leading the project. They must be meeting their career goals. This is the measure of a remarkable construction project, and so in this brief section, I want to go through each of these and redefine what success looks like for us.

Number one is safety. Safety is a mindset. Safety has the measurement of perfection, and it can't have another measurement. We can't be excellent or good enough for safety because we can't accidentally kill somebody and then double-check them and make it alright. We only get one shot at this. We have to have perfection when it comes to safety and the well-being of our people. It's a mindset, and I can promise you that ninety-five percent of the people reading this book have their set point where safety is set to around sixty to seventy-five percent on the excellent scale, but we need something well above ninety percent if we're going to actually keep people safe. When I'm talking about safety, what I mean is that it's the first thing on your mind, it's the first thing that you check, it's the first thing that you think of in the morning. It's the first thing that you do, it's the first thing that you ensure, it's the priority, it's the principle, it's the value, it's whatever you want to call it, but it is always on your mind and annoyingly and naggingly, you can never get rid of it. If you are not annoying other people with your focus on safety, then you don't yet get it. Until you understand that the lives and well-being of every single person on the project are up to you and your standards, you don't fully understand what it means to be a leader. Until you feel the burden and the weight of everybody's lives and the lives of their family, then you are not ready to lead out with safety on your project.

The second one is quality. Quality is the way you run the project, and it is the measurement of a great project. You cannot have a project finished on time and safely if it is not built in a quality manner. We have to do everything in a quality manner and when we do, it will elevate safety, our schedule, and production as well. You cannot have good team health, good safety, good production, and a good schedule if you don't also have good quality. They are all interconnected.

The third measure of success is to understand that production is about creating capacity. As you've already learned, production has nothing to do with pushing. It has nothing to do with randomly adding manpower or randomly adding materials and delivering them to the project site. It has nothing to do with spending money and throwing costs and money at the problem. It has nothing to do with rushing or pushing workers to go too fast. Nor does success have anything to do with making people do out of sequence work or overextending themselves. Production comes from creating flow for the trades. If the trades are not making money and in a good flow, and if you do not have good production, then you also do not have a good plan and overall schedule duration. To have a good project, you must have good production with your trades.

Fourth, the team must be high functioning, healthy, and happy. The team has to enjoy working there. There has to be a good feel in the trailer and on the project site. There has to be good morale. The foremen, whether it's a difficult job or not, should love working there. It is the project supers, the senior supers, and the general superintendent's job to make sure that there are high levels of morale on the project site which again, affects the quality, production, and safety of everything else on the project site.

Additionally, we must have a raving fan customer. That customer is paying us to do a job—not only for the end product—but for the production system throughout. I once heard of an owner of a construction company saying, "I want to deliver what we sell." The production system that produces the building is just as remarkable as the end product. If you were to go into a BMW manufacturing plant to look at the beautiful end product, could you go on the assembly line and see how they assemble them and be just as impressed? That is the goal of having a raving fan customer along the way. Are they happy? Do they feel like we are taking care of their needs? Do they feel like the project is clean, safe, and organized? Do you feel the neighbors are taken care of? Do they feel like they are represented well? Are we making it easy for them to manage their risk, be adaptable, and nimble to changes.

One time the Vice President of Planning and Design for a university came on to our construction project and said, "When I come here, the morale, the excitement, the energy, and the fun things that I get to see make me feel like I'm going to Disneyland." This was a part of a normal project tour which was a surprise to the workers when the daily operations on-site were remarkable enough that we created not only raving fan customers, but an enjoyable environment where the project team and the customers had fun together.

The other measure of success is when the people on the project site are meeting their career goals and actually getting to take that next step. Is that project engineer getting to do PM tasks? Is that field engineer getting to do assistant superintendent tasks? Is that foreman getting to do field engineering tasks? Everyone must be growing and progressing in their career on the job as well.

And lastly, schedule. A project must finish on schedule in an even flow, and if it's not possible and there are circumstances beyond your control, that schedule must be extended so we don't push workers.

In conclusion, a project is only successful if it's safe and built in a quality manner, each trade partner is productive and making money, the team is high functioning and happy, we're caring for the customers and providing a remarkable experience, we have raving fans, everyone on the project is meeting their career goals, and we finish on time. You, as a leader, as a project senior or general superintendent, are awarded no points and get no credit for any project that does not meet all of those criteria. That is the minimum criteria for finishing with a successful project. You have to elevate your standards and adhere to that level of success and that definition of success as we head into the principles or the steps that you will follow to implement operational excellence on your project. This is the way!

THE ART OF THE BUILDER

The Books

I will now refer to the books that make up this work. They are listed below.

High-Performance Habits: How Extraordinary People Become That Way by Brendon Burchard:

In this book, Brendan Burchard explains the six high-performance habits that effective leaders must master to succeed. If you struggle with clarity, energy, necessity, productivity, influence, or courage, I highly recommend you pick up this book.

Leadership and Self-Deception: Getting Out of the Box by The Arbinger Institute:

Every superintendent should read this book. In this work, you will learn how to *get out of the box*. That is an expression that describes how we can leave the metaphorical box of self-deception we allow when we become triggered, assume negative intent, and engage in unhealthy interpersonal interactions. This book provides guidance for breaking that pattern and reframing every difficult situation so that we can do the right thing and remain in control of our emotions.

How to Win Friends and Influence People by Dale Carnegie:

This book will help you develop your interpersonal skills. It was initially written as a lecture series about how to deal with people. It is well-written with illustrative stories in every section. Many have found this book life-changing and immediately implementable, and I hope you will too.

The Speed of Trust: The One Thing that Changes Everything by Stephen R. Covey, et al.:

Have you ever wondered what it takes for someone to trust you? Would you like to know? Character and competence. A person must know your intentions, character, track record, and abilities. Stephen R. Covey outlines a pattern of behavior for us that we can use to build trust which is the first step in team building.

It's Your Ship: Management Techniques from the Best Damn Ship in the Navy by Captain D. Michael Abrashoff:

In this wonderful read, Captain D. Michael Abrashoff takes you through the story of leading the crew on the USS Benfold. I think superintendents should read this because it showcases the ownership, creativity, and high standards any leader can have when directing their project or ship.

Extreme Ownership: How U.S. Navy SEALs Lead and Win by Jocko Willink and Leif Babin:

If you have ever struggled with any form of a victim mentality, consider reading this book. They provide examples from experience on deployment about how to be accountable, own the mission, and move forward as a competent team leader.

The Goal: A Process of Ongoing Improvement by Eliyahu M. Goldratt:

This book provides the basis for creating flow in manufacturing and must be translated to construction so we can focus on flow.

The Bottleneck Rules: The Go-To Guide to Eli Goldratt's Theory of Constraints (TOC) and his Business Novel 'The Goal' (Theory of Constraints Simplified) by Clarke Ching:

This book does a nice job of simplifying the novel *The Goal*. It discusses in detail how to identify and optimize bottlenecks on a project.

This is Lean: Resolving the Efficiency Paradox by Niklas Modig and Par Ahlstrom:
This is the best book about Lean and Lean concepts on the market. Every superintendent in our industry–and every person for that matter–should read this book.

Toyota Production System: Beyond Large-scale Production by Taiichi Ohno:
If a superintendent wants to understand the foundations of Lean and the difference between flow and pull, this book is a must-read.

The Lean Builder: A Builder's Guide to Applying Lean Tools in the Field by Joe Donarumo and Keyan Zandy:
This excellent book summarizes how to implement the Last Planner® system in construction.

Scrum: The Art of Doing Twice the Work in Half the Time by Jeff and J.J. Sutherland:
This is an exceptional book summarizing how to implement Scrum as a scheduling system.

2 Second Lean: How to Grow People and Build a Fun Lean Culture by Paul A. Akers:
In *2 Second Lean,* Paul Akers teaches the process of implementing Lean principles that have worked for him in his manufacturing facility. The concepts do not tie exactly to construction but can be applied to any leadership situation. He leads the reader through the process of creating a Lean culture of excellence. He simplifies it so that anyone can understand and does it in an interesting and abbreviated form. We recommend everyone study this book a few times to be sure to absorb the message.

Elevating Construction Superintendents: A Principle Based Leadership Guide for Assistant Supers and Superintendents in Construction (The Art of The Builder) by Jason Schroeder:
This is fundamental to understanding how a superintendent can approach their role in construction.

Takt Planning & Integrated Control: A Fable and Instructional Guide about Creating Stability and Flow on Projects with The Takt Production System Supported by Last Planner® and Scrum by Jason Schroeder with Spencer Easton:
CPM is not the best scheduling method in construction. This book outlines how to create, implement, and use Takt planning in construction as the master scheduling system.

Multipliers, Revised and Updated: How the Best Leaders Make Everyone Smarter by Liz Wiseman, John Meagher, et al.:
This is a must for a leader focused on becoming better at their job. There are multipliers and diminishers in this world. Diminishers don't believe in people and micromanage. Multipliers believe in people and multiply their efforts!

Mindset: The New Psychology of Success by Carol Dweck:
This is likely the most important book of the century. It outlines the difference between a growth and fixed mindset. Every leader should read this book so they can adopt a growth mindset and really thrive in their career.

Essentialism: The Disciplined Pursuit of Less by Greg McKeown:
This book is crucial for leaders that feel overwhelmed. A senior super must focus on what is essential, and this book will help with that focus.

How to Stop Worrying and Start Living by Dale Carnegie:
In How to Stop Worrying and Start Living, Dale Carnegie again provides advice that has no equal in the form of how

to reduce stress and worry. For those who tend to suffer from stress and anxiety, the practical steps he lists in the book can make the difference between a happy and productive life and one of constant misery.

The Upside of Stress: Why Stress Is Good for You, and How to Get Good at It by Kelly McGonigal:
There is good stress and bad stress. This book will help any leader identify the difference and move as much of the pressure as possible from the stressful category to the helpful.

The Life-Changing Magic of Tidying Up: The Japanese Art of Decluttering and Organizing by Marie Kondo:
In this book, Marie Kondo explains the Japanese philosophy of practicing cleanliness and organization in an effort to strive for perfection. It is hard for people to understand the need for cleanliness on projects in this industry. That is because we are all conditioned for mediocrity. With her passionate approach to tidying, Kondo can inspire the reader to reach for perfection and joy in cleaning. Everything on-site should bring joy to the workers, owners, and management team. She will show you how.

33 Strategies of War by Robert Greene:
As a superintendent, I really appreciated this book about military strategy. However, some chapters do not apply—for instance, the chapters about espionage. If a Super reads this with a selective eye, they will glean wisdom from indispensable history.

The Art of War by Sun Tzu:
Most everyone knows this is a classic for any leader interested in logistics, strategy, and tactics.

The Motive: Why So Many Leaders Abdicate Their Most Important Responsibilities by Patrick M. Lencioni:
This book is remarkably clear about what leaders should focus on so they do not abdicate what only a leader can and should do.

The Five Dysfunctions of a Team: A Leadership Fable by Patrick M. Lencioni:
This book is essential for anyone who is part of a team or leads one. Every team will struggle if they do not apply the principles of building trust and employing healthy conflict. It's hard to believe, but the answer to how we can be a good team is simple and contained in this book.

Death by Meeting: A Leadership Fable...About Solving the Most Painful Problem in Business by Patrick M. Lencioni:
This book will help any leader run a remarkable meeting.

The Advantage: Why Organizational Health Trumps Everything Else In Business by Patrick M. Lencioni:
This book shows how scaling communication is key to any leadership position and team.

The Truth About Employee Engagement: A Fable About Addressing the Three Root Causes of Job Misery by Patrick M. Lencioni:
This book will help you as a leader to be a good manager and create engagement with your direct reports.

The Ideal Team Player: How to Recognize and Cultivate the Three Essential Virtues by Patrick M. Lencioni:
Patrick Lencioni demonstrates the need to be humble, hungry, and smart to be an ideal team player. You may think you know what those words mean, but there is much more to each of them than what initially comes to mind. The book's message is helpful, insightful, and life-changing if applied.

The Toyota Way: 14 Management Principles from the World's Greatest Manufacturer by Jeffrey Liker:
The 14 principles in this book are crucial to Lean construction implementations. Jeffrey outlines the key principles that will support and benefit any construction project.

The Leader Who Had No Title: A Modern Fable on Real Success in Business and in Life by Robin Sharma:

This book is a little corny, but it clearly identifies in a simple manner what steps each leader should take to give and develop influence.

The Go-giver: A Little Story About a Powerful Business Idea by John David Mann and Bob Burg:

This book changed my life. Every leader must focus on giving to be ultimately successful. This book will help change your perspective so you can provide more and lead the way you want.

Switch: How to Change Things When Change is Hard by Chip and Dan Heath:

Switch was written to help people with implementation. If you have already learned the art of dealing with people, the next step is to find safe and effective ways to lead individuals and groups through the process of change. The authors take the reader through a thought-provoking analogy of the Rider, the Elephant, and the Path. The Rider is our intellect, the Elephant is our motivation, and the Path represents our circumstances when trying to change. All three must work together. Chip and Dan Heath provide practical steps to help us implement change when it becomes hard. The book is important because it will allow builders to become adept at implementing change on projects. Without this practical knowledge, it can be easy to fall victim to unavoidable circumstances.

The Captain Class: The Hidden Force That Creates the World's Greatest Teams by Sam Walker:

This book shows how any leader can support and enable their team for optimum performance.

I hope you enjoy these books as I have. If you don't like

reading actual books, consider Kindle. If that does not work for you, consider Audible. If Audible does not work for you, a service called Blinkist summarizes these books for you into Blinks that total around ten minutes of listening time.

Conclusion

Every structure must have a foundation. The foundation of a construction project is not the concrete footings; it is the team that will organize and build it. Every project must have the right team to be successful. I hope you are now better equipped to build a team and lead a team. This will set up all remaining success you will have on a construction project. Where is your time best spent? Building the job? Or building the team (including yourself) that will build the job? I hope the answer to this is now obvious. Ultimately, if you feel you are better able to create healthy and balanced environments and if you feel you have a path to improve yourself as the captain of your ship, then I think this work has served a purpose for you. If it has, please reach out to me if you ever need help or training. Please help me scale systems and training that will bring respect back to construction, improve the lives of builders, and protect families at home.

At its core, a Lean system has respect for people and then the two pillars of people and process. This book was about people, and the next book will be about process. In book two we will learn the systems you will implement on a project to achieve remarkable operational results. I hope you will join me with book two when it and you are ready. Until we meet again, please rate this work highly, review it, and share it with your colleagues so we can scale the message that construction can be remarkable, fun, and rewarding. In our industry we have all the knowledge we need to run remarkable projects; the key now is to scale that information.

And lastly, I want you to know that I think about you when I am writing at home, on the plane, or late at night. I truly care about you and this industry.

On we go!
Jason

THE END of Book 1

Made in the USA
Coppell, TX
29 January 2026

69696069R00137